Charles Wesley (1707–1788) Preacher, Poet, Pastor

Special Issue of
*The Journal of Religious History,
Literature and Culture*
2024

Papers presented at the 29th annual meeting of
the Charles Wesley Society at John Wesley's New Room,
Bristol, 9–11 August 2018

Edited by
CLIVE MURRAY NORRIS

Volume 10 November 2024 N
UNIVERSITY OF WALES PRESS
https://doi.org/10.16922/jrhlc.10.2

Editors
Professor William Gibson, Oxford Brookes University
Professor John Morgan-Guy, University of Wales Trinity Saint David
Dr Daniel Reed, Oxford Brookes University

Assistant Editor
Dr Thomas W. Smith, Rugby School

Reviews Editor
Dr Nicky Tsougarakis, University of Crete

Editorial Advisory Board
Professor David Bebbington, Stirling University
Professor Stewart J. Brown, University of Edinburgh
Dr James J. Caudle, Yale University
Rt Revd J. Wyn Evans
Dr Robert G. Ingram, University of Florida, USA
Professor Geraint Jenkins, Aberystwyth University
Dr David Ceri Jones, Aberystwyth University
Dr Paul Kerry, Brigham Young University, USA
Professor Frances Knight, University of Nottingham
Dr Robert Pope, Westminster College, Cambridge
Professor Huw Pryce, Bangor University
Emeritus Professor Kenneth E. Roxburgh, Samford University, USA
Dr Eryn M. White, Aberystwyth University
Rt Revd and Rt Hon. Lord Williams of Oystermouth
Professor Jonathan Wooding, University of Sydney, Australia

Editorial Contacts
wgibson@brookes.ac.uk
d.reed@brookes.ac.uk
thomas.smith.2009@live.rhul.ac.uk
Tsougarakis@uoc.gr

CONTENTS

The Contributors   v

Editorial
Clive Murray Norris   vii

Charles Wesley's Role in the Formative Early Years in Bristol,
1739–41
Gary M. Best   1

Songs of Renewal: The language of renewal in the hymns
of Charles Wesley
Paul W. Chilcote   21

Charles Wesley and Archaic Symbolism
Pauline Watson   43

Music and Charles Wesley's Legacy
Martin V. Clarke   57

Portraits of Charles Wesley (1707–88)
Peter S. Forsaith   81

'From all the arts of hell secure': Charles Wesley's relationship
to John Henderson (1757–88)
Jonathan Barry   97

Index   114

THE CONTRIBUTORS

Jonathan Barry is emeritus professor of history at Exeter University, and guest professor in early modern history at LMU in Munich. He is co-editor of the Bristol Record Society and of Palgrave Historical Studies in Witchcraft and Magic and Palgrave Studies in Medieval and Early Modern Medicine.

Gary M. Best was headmaster of Kingswood School for twenty-one years and then served as lay warden of the New Room in Bristol 2009–19, creating its new much-praised Wesley Museum and its new Visitor Centre. He has published twenty books, including biographies of Charles Wesley, Grace Murray, and John Cennick, and histories of the New Room, Kingswood School, and Bristol's role in the slave trade.

Paul W. Chilcote serves in retirement as a research fellow of Wesley House, Cambridge. Author of more than thirty books, he has published broadly in Wesleyan studies, with specialization on Charles and John Wesley and early Methodist women. His two award-winning titles related to Charles Wesley are *Singing the Faith: Soundings of Lyrical Theology in the Methodist Tradition* (2020) and *A Faith That Sings: Biblical Themes in the Lyrical Theology of Charles Wesley* (2016).

Martin V. Clarke is a senior lecturer in music at the Open University. He has published widely on Methodist hymnody and Welsh music history, including *British Methodist Hymnody: Theology, Heritage, and Experience* (2018) and *A History of Welsh Music* (co-edited with Trevor Herbert and Helen Barlow, 2023).

Peter Forsaith is a historian specialising in culture, religion and society in later eighteenth and early nineteenth century Britain though he is also interested in architecture and historic buildings. He holds a PhD, is a Fellow of the Royal Historical Society and is based in Oxford.

Clive Murray Norris is a historian of early Methodism, specializing in its finances and organisation. He co-edited *The Routledge Handbook* *to John Wesley* (2023) and is secretary of the UK branch of the Charles Wesley Society.

Pauline Watson graduated in medicine from Glasgow University and holds a PhD in Theology from Durham University. She has worked as a general practitioner, a psychiatrist and a psychoanalytic psychotherapist.

EDITORIAL

Charles Wesley (1707–88), younger brother of the more celebrated John, is now recognised not only as a superlative writer of sacred verse but as one of the founders of what developed into the global Methodist movement of some eighty million people. In 2018, members of the Charles Wesley Society met in Bristol to review aspects of his life and work. These essays are based on papers offered to that meeting, which took place in the historic Methodist chapel known as the New Room. I am grateful to our contributors for reviewing their papers and updating them as necessary. Taken together, they present Charles as a preacher, poet, and pastor.

The volume opens with Gary Best's account of early Methodism in Bristol, for which the New Room was a key centre. This situates Charles Wesley primarily as an evangelist and church leader. From late 1739 he began to preach in Bristol and the surrounding area, following the initiatives launched first by George Whitefield and then by John Wesley. Unlike his brother John, Charles tended to preach without notes, offering his hearers a straightforward path to salvation, and contemporary accounts attest to the impact of this simple gospel message, which often attracted large and enthusiastic crowds. However, his efforts also drew significant and sometimes violent opposition, and Charles needed all the spiritual and physical strength he could muster to maintain them.

There was also tension between Charles and Whitefield and another active preacher, the layman John Cennick, partly because of the Wesleys' aversion to Whitefield's Calvinism, and partly because of John Wesley's distinctive doctrine of Christian perfection. By January 1741 these problems were seriously undermining the overall evangelistic campaign in Bristol; in February, John Wesley expelled Cennick from membership in his 'connexion', and many of the rank and file left with him. Charles, however, sought to continue the brothers' joint enterprise with the Calvinists and his conciliatory approach reduced the potential damage caused by John's stridency. The essay illuminates Charles's central role in this turbulent and formative period of Methodism's history.

Paul Chilcote's essay treats of Charles in his more familiar persona of Methodism's pre-eminent hymnwriter. We talk perhaps glibly of the

https://doi.org/10.16922/jrhlc.10.2.1

eighteenth-century evangelical 'revival', but when Charles used this and cognate words in his hymns what exactly did he mean? In some 20 per cent of hymns in the Wesleys' seminal 1780 *Collection*, Charles uses forms of the verbs 'restore', 'renew' and 'revive': the concepts pervade the hymnal. His core message is that three related and precious promises are on offer to those seeking salvation: 'the restoration of perfect love in the child of God, the recovery of God's rule, and the revival of the church as God's instrument of renewal in the world.'

Each of these core concepts is itself developed extensively in Charles's corpus. Thus 'restoration' appears in terms of the restoration of the sinner's heart to wholeness, the reinstatement of the image of God in the believer, and the display of Christ-like love in the believer's life. But Charles has a wider vision, of the establishment of God's kingdom on earth, one of justice and peace. For example, he writes extensively in his hymns of the poor, calling for practical acts of compassion towards the widow and the orphan. He also eagerly anticipates the New Heaven and New Earth which would be inaugurated by the Second Coming of Jesus Christ. Finally, Charles's concept of 'revival' places a clear responsibility upon the church, and specifically on those enlisting in the Methodist movement, to recover the simple faith and practice of the early followers of Jesus. In some hymns he urged the Church of England to reform; in others he welcomed the signs that Methodists were indeed rediscovering the spirituality of the early church. But throughout his ministry of word and song Charles Wesley urged his hearers to participate in a revival which was breathtaking in scope, encompassing their own behaviour, peace and justice in the wider world, and ultimately the renewal of all creation.

Pauline Watson's essay looks beyond the language of Charles's hymns to the Christian symbols which they deploy. She argues that the hymns take us beyond ourselves in two ways, by opening us up to the transcendent and by reconnecting us with our early selves. Charles Wesley generates depth and complexity of meaning through techniques including the use of metaphor, neologisms, and paradox, in often strikingly condensed phrases. These point us towards deep theological truths, as in one thirty-five word summary of the nature of and relationships between the three persons of the Trinity.

Often, Charles's use of language about the believer's path to salvation also echoes, at a deep but perhaps unconscious level, the infant's epic struggle to establish independence and self-understanding on leaving

Editorial

the security of the mother's womb. The powerful feelings experienced in early life, especially if unresolved, can have long-term and possibly damaging consequences. This prompts the obvious question, which Watson then addresses, of the extent to which the Wesley brothers were moulded by their experience in infancy.

Her argument is that Charles had an easier early life than John and was thus more ready to use imagery which recalled the visceral struggles of the infant for survival and sustenance, physical and emotional. John, in contrast, was uncomfortable with the emphasis on Christ's blood and wounds, as found amongst the Moravians. In conclusion, she suggests that this differential, early personal history may explain the continuing power of Charles's hymns to move us – beyond words.

Martin Clarke's essay examines the music to which Charles Wesley's hymns were and are sung, reminding us of their multiple roles in forging a collective Methodist identity as well as nurturing individual seekers and adherents. A significant number of his hymns, albeit a small proportion of the estimated nine thousand he wrote, have been widely and continuously sung in worship by Methodists and other Christians in Great Britain and beyond since the eighteenth century. Charles's hymn texts were written to be sung, whether by the early followers of Methodism in the small group meetings that were integral to the movement's structure, or in the public worship of the Church of England, which the early Methodist leaders sought to reinvigorate. Most people, within and beyond Methodism, who have encountered Charles Wesley's religious poetry since the mid-eighteenth century have done so through participating in hymn singing or by hearing others do so.

Drawing on case studies of especially celebrated hymns by Charles, Clarke examines the complexity of the relationship between words and music in his hymns. The mood and tone of a hymn can change across its stanzas, while the tune is fixed; on the other hand, a single piece of verse can be twinned with multiple tunes. Charles had a wide-ranging musical education, and this is reflected in the range of metres in which he wrote hymns; he was also a metrical innovator. Some tunes used by early Methodists had their origins in the London theatre, suggesting a contested relationship with the seriousness of the hymns' messages. However, by the early nineteenth century Methodists increasingly sang Charles's hymns to simple and emphatic tunes, embodying the 'spirited singing' for which Methodist congregations were then known. Later in the century, growing Methodist respectability found its reflection in the choice of hymn-tunes, as have – more recently – 'ecumenical opportunities and tensions'. Even today Charles's words continue to inspire composers working in contemporary idioms, as well as congregations across the world.

Peter Forsaith's contribution moves away from words and music to explain how Charles has been portrayed visually in his lifetime and later. He notes the paradox that 'Charles Wesley, who moved in cultural and artistic circles, should have so few portraits compared to his brother John, who eschewed such company'. While there are contemporary portraits at least ostensibly from the life, his posthumous portrayals have typically been in heroic style, celebrating one of the founding fathers of Methodism.

In our final essay, Jonathan Barry throws light upon Charles's relationship with the brilliant but eccentric John Henderson (1757–88); Charles here features primarily as a pastor. Henderson was a minor eighteenth-century celebrity, and leading figures ranging from Samuel Johnson to Edmund Burke and William Wilberforce tried (but failed) to establish him in a career suited to his prodigious talents. Charles Wesley took a close – indeed paternal – interest in John, writing seven hymns reflecting his aimless life and urging God to lead him into a more productive path, 'From all the *arts of hell* secure'. This was a reference to John Henderson's interest in magic and the occult, an interest which (surprisingly) he shared with the leading Methodist scholar and minister Adam Clarke.

Since Henderson died at thirty-two, one can only speculate what contribution he might have made had he followed his father into the Methodist ministry. He benefited from Charles's pastoral ministry but failed to find his way; a reminder to historians that great talent does not always flourish, and that much of the life and work of significant figures such as Charles Wesley was in fact devoted to these personal encounters which are largely missing from the historical record and thus not visible to our gaze.

CLIVE MURRAY NORRIS

CHARLES WESLEY'S ROLE IN THE FORMATIVE EARLY YEARS IN BRISTOL, 1739–41

Gary M. Best

This essay situates Charles Wesley primarily as an evangelist and church leader and illuminates his central role in this turbulent and formative period of Methodism's history. From late 1739 Charles began to preach in Bristol and the surrounding area, following the initiatives launched first by George Whitefield and then by John Wesley. He offered his hearers a straightforward path to salvation, and often attracted large and enthusiastic crowds. However, his efforts also drew significant and sometimes violent opposition, and there was also tension between Charles and Whitefield and another active preacher, the layman John Cennick, partly because of the Wesleys' aversion to Whitefield's Calvinism, and partly because of John Wesley's distinctive doctrine of Christian perfection. By January 1741 these problems were seriously undermining the overall evangelistic campaign in Bristol, leading to a split within the movement. Charles, however, sought to continue the brothers' joint enterprise with the Calvinists and took a conciliatory approach.

Keywords: Charles Wesley, Bristol, Methodism, Evangelical Revival, Calvinism

Traditional accounts of early Methodism usually describe how George Whitefield commenced preaching in the open air first to the colliers at Kingswood and then to large crowds in Bristol before handing over control of the revival to John Wesley. Charles's role is often either understated or omitted altogether. I hope to remedy that in this account. But first let me say a few things about John and his work in Bristol. Unlike George Whitefield, John was initially an unknown figure to Bristolians,

https://doi.org/10.16922/jrhlc.10.2.2

and, as a consequence, he drew much smaller crowds. Those that came to hear him did so either out of curiosity or because of the praise which Whitefield had lavished on John in advance of his arrival. Mary Thomas, one of those who went to hear Wesley, later wrote: 'I heard . . . [Mr Whitefield] telling that there was one coming after him whose shoelaces he was not worthy to unloose'.[1] Doubtless as John's confidence grew so did the quality of his preaching and, by his reckoning, about fifty thousand people came to hear him within the first month of his being in Bristol. However, John drew that number of people not entirely by his oratory. What contributed to the attraction of going to hear him were the emotional scenes that accompanied his very different style of preaching. Whitefield had often reduced a crowd to tears, but John took delight in people shouting and swearing and shrieking and moaning. John Cennick, there to assist John, was horrified by the behaviour John encouraged:

> I have seen people so foam and be violently agitated that six men could not hold one, but he would spring out of their arms or off the ground, and tear himself as in hellish agonies. Others I have seen sweat uncommonly and their necks and tongues swell and twist out of all shape. Some prophesied, and some uttered the worst of blasphemies against our Saviour.[2]

When George Whitefield visited Bristol in the summer he was impressed by what the increasingly confident John was achieving:

> I found that Bristol had great reason to bless God for the ministry of Mr John Wesley. The congregations I observed to be much more serious and affected than when I had left them . . . [And in Kingswood] a great and visible alteration is seen in the behaviour of the colliers. Instead of cursing and swearing, they are heard to sing hymns about the woods; and the rising generation, I hope, will be a generation of Christians.[3]

But he was not happy about John's preaching technique:

> I cannot think it right in you to give so much encouragement to those convulsions which people have been thrown into under your ministry . . . The devil. I believe, doth interpose. I think it will

> encourage . . . people . . . [to] depend on visions, convulsions, etc more than on the promises and precepts of the gospel.[4]

The approach adopted by John was sensationalist and it pulled in crowds, but it is no surprise that the clergy in Bristol took umbrage to it. It is why the Bishop of Bristol, who had given official permission for Whitefield to preach, decided he had to call Wesley before him in August and condemn what he was doing as 'a very horrid thing', saying 'Mr. Wesley, I will deal plainly with you. I once thought Mr. Whitefield and you well-meaning men. But I can't think so now'.[5] The Bishop was also unhappy because John was permitting a layman, John Cennick, to address the colliers in Kingswood. John's decision to do so had been taken against the advice of Whitefield, who thought Cennick too young and unqualified.

This was the situation when Charles Wesley arrived in Bristol twelve days later on 28 August and took up residence in the home of George Whitefield's sister in Wine Street. He spent a couple of days familiarising himself with the city and getting to meet key society members and wrote afterwards: 'We were all of one heart and mind . . . I felt all at once into the strictest intimacy with these delightful souls, and could not forebear saying, "It is good for me to be here".'[6] He heard his brother preach to society members at the New Room before John headed off for London on 31 August and left Charles in charge. By this stage Charles was, of course, already experienced in the art of speaking in the open, not just because of his time in America, but because, since 24 June, he had been doing that in London and the Cotswolds. The experience had removed, in his words, all his earlier 'doubts and scruples' and left him in no doubt that God wanted him to preach in the open: 'God shone upon my path, and I knew this was his will concerning me'.[7]

In London, Charles had drawn much bigger crowds than John had attracted in Bristol. Indeed, I suspect that Whitefield had intended that Charles should stay on as his successor in London. It was John who determined that he should speak in the capital and Charles in Bristol. Charles preached for the first time in the open air in Bristol on 1 September. He spoke at five o'clock in the morning at the Bowling Green. He says he 'called all the early and heavy-laden to Christ', that 'none offered to go away though it rained hard', and that 'the hearers appeared deeply affected'.[8] Thereafter, he commenced preaching in the other venues which had been used by Whitefield and his brother. This included preaching for the first time to 'some thousands' of the colliers on 4 September in

Kingswood, where he says 'I triumphed in God's mercy to these poor outcasts'.[9] The following day he refers to praying with John Cennick for those colliers who were not behaving as they should.

One senses from his journal that almost immediately Charles felt his preaching was making the right kind of impact. For example, on the 7 September he says: 'God was with my mouth. I preached and prayed believing'; on the 8th: 'never did I see the like power among us'; on the 9th: 'I never spoke more searchingly'; and on the 10th: 'It rained hard yet none stirred. I spoke with great freedom and power'. Opposition did not deter him. He wrote after facing considerable heckling from a hostile section of a very large crowd at an open-air event at the Bowling Green on 16 September: 'I lifted up my voice like a trumpet, and in a few minutes, drove him [i.e. the Devil] out of the field. For above an hour I preached the Gospel with extraordinary power'.[10]

From the few accounts that we have, it would appear that Charles's preaching was different from that of John, less dry and more emotional in terms of its delivery. Whereas John relied on notes prepared in advance, Charles preferred preaching extempore.[11] The preacher John Nelson, for example, commented in 1742 that when he heard Charles, 'the Lord was with him in such manner that the pillars of hell seemed to tremble'.[12] The preacher John Valton, hearing Charles preach in 1764, wrote: 'His word was with power; and I thought my Saviour was at hand, never being so sensibly affected under a discourse before'.[13] Another preacher, Joseph Sutcliffe, heard Charles when he was very old and frail and commented: 'Age and infirmities were left behind. It was a torrent of exhortation and eloquence bearing down all before him'.[14] John Whitehead, the first official biographer of John Wesley, heard both the brothers preach, and he regarded Charles's sermons to be more 'awakening and useful' than his brother's:

> His discourses from the pulpit were not dry and systematic, but flowed from the present views and feelings of his own mind. He had a remarkable talent of expressing the most important truths with simplicity and energy; and his discourses were sometimes truly apostolic, forcing conviction on his hearers in spite of the most determined opposition.[15]

According to Charles, his favourite theme in these early days of preaching in Bristol was justification by faith. The accounts of Mary

Thomas and Margaret Austin, two of the women who heard Charles preach, are particularly interesting because they provide a comparison between his preaching and that of George Whitefield and John Wesley. Mary Thomas says she 'very much approved' of what Whitefield preached and that his recommendation of John Wesley had predisposed her to have 'great love in her heart' for him. However, when she heard John preach, it left her with 'nothing but discontent in my mind' because he made her feel so very sinful. She preferred listening to Charles because his manner of speaking was 'far finer' than that of his brother, and, although he had made her feel equally sinful, he had also guided her until she was able to experience the assurance of salvation.[16] Margaret Austin gives a similar picture:

> [I was] Awakened by the Reverend Mr. Whitefield: Convicted by the Reverend Mr. John Wesley: Converted by the Reverend Mr. Charles: for the truth of whose Doctrine in the Strength of the Lord I am ready to lay down my Life.[17]

As early as 3 September, Charles makes reference to having discourse with a gentleman who was offended at 'the cryings out'.[18] In response he was initially defensive of his brother and he appears to have tolerated the behaviour of those who were shouting out or fainting, but increasingly he came to view the highly emotional behaviour as just a mixture of attention-seeking and delusional folly. He therefore soon refused to accept it. Within three weeks his reputation as a preacher was earning him invitations to other towns. The most famous account of his preaching style comes from the pen of the Calvinist dissenter Joseph Williams, who travelled down from Kidderminster in early October to hear him because of the reports he had heard of Charles's brilliance as a preacher:

> I got a guide and went to hear him. I found him standing on a table-board, in an erect posture, with his hands and eyes lifted up to heaven in prayer, surrounded with, I guess, more than a thousand people; some few of them fashionable ... but most of the lower rank of mankind ... He prayed with uncommon fervency, fluency, and variety of proper expression. He then preached about an hour ... in such a manner as I have seldom, if ever, heard any Minister preach ... to convince his hearers that ... God is willing to be reconciled to all, even the worst of sinners. Although he used

no notes, nor had anything in his hand but a Bible, yet he delivered his thoughts in a rich, copious variety of expressions, and with so much propriety that I could not observe anything incoherent, or inaccurate through the whole performance, which he concluded with singing, prayer, and the usual benediction . . . Never did I see or hear such fervency in the service of God . . . If there be such a thing as heavenly music upon earth, I heard it there . . . I do not remember my heart to have been so elevated, either in collegiate, parochial, or private worship, as it was there and then . . . If, therefore, any inquire . . . 'Can any good come out of Methodism?' I can only answer . . . 'Come and see'.[19]

In the first fortnight of his new role in Bristol, Charles makes a few references to some health issues arising from the workload. Preaching in the open and to societies, speaking with the society bands and with individuals, travelling, and dealing with pastoral matters, including tending the sick and dying – it all meant very busy and long days. The physical impact made him feel he was not up to the task, especially as he tended to be highly self-critical of himself:

I always find strength for the work of the ministry; but when my work is over, my strength, both bodily and spiritual, leaves me. I can pray for others, not for myself. God by me strengthens the weak hands, and confirms the feeble knees; yet am I myself as a man in whom is no strength. I am weary and faint in my mind, longing continually to be discharged.[20]

What made his work more difficult was that he had inherited a situation where the opposition to Methodism was ever-increasing. At the end of his first month in the city he wrote:

Christianity flourishes under the cross. None who follow after Christ want that badge of discipleship. Wives and children are beaten, and turned out of doors; and the persecutors are the complainers . . . Every Sunday damnation is denounced against all that hear us Papists, us Jesuits, us seducers, us bringers in of the Pretender. The Clergy murmur aloud at the number of communicants, and threaten to repel them; yet will not the world bear that we should talk of persecution . . . Some lose their bread, some their habitations; one suffers stripes, another confinement; and yet we must not call this persecution. Doubtless they will find some other name for it, when they do God service by killing us.[21]

What comes across in Charles's journal is the extent to which he drew comfort and strength to continue from receiving the positive feedback of individuals and from seeing his opponents often overcome. Here for example is an extract from his journal for 1 October:

> Many find power to believe, either in or soon after hearing . . . In the afternoon I went out into the lanes and streets of the city . . . The power of the Lord accompanied me . . . At Gloucester Lane, while I discoursed on 'the man born blind' three Pharisees lay concealed at an house adjoining; and they could not have come at a more convenient season. God was with my mouth. They could not stand it, but made their escape in the middle of my discourse. The sincere were strengthened and comforted, as several testified at that time.[22]

Even more apparent is the extent to which he relied on prayer to sustain him. On 19 September, for example, he describes how at a meeting with the male bands neither he nor his audience were in the right frame of mind. The atmosphere was 'weak, spiritless, dead' and he goes on to say:

> I wanted to get away without speaking or praying, because they were all as dead, it seemed, as I. I was overruled to stay and pray, and had the spirit of prayer as never before. We were all in a flame; I prayed again and again, not knowing how to part.[23]

On 7 October, Charles went for communion to St Philip's Church and wrote:

> I first earnestly asked that God would not send me empty away. I returned to my pew, and was immediately overpowered, in a manner inexpressible . . . with the strongest assurance that I should receive all I wait for. God mollified my hardness, and I abhorred myself before him, as in dust and ashes. I asked, with all submission, some token from his word. I hardly remember to have read the passage: it came with power, and abased me to nothing: 'Thou art my battle-axe, and weapons of war; for in thee will I break in pieces the nations'.[24]

Nevertheless, Charles required as much support as he could get and there is no doubt that he quickly forged a good relationship with John Cennick. It is quite clear from Cennick's writings that he preferred Charles's approach to preaching to that of John Wesley. Cennick hated John's encouragement of weird behaviour and he appears to have willingly accepted Charles as his preaching mentor. So much was this the case that when John Wesley visited Bristol and Kingswood in mid-October, Cennick had the temerity to inform him that he could no longer view the emotional behaviour of crowds and society members as being the work of God. As far as he was concerned, he had 'no doubt but the whole was delusion'.[25] John insisted that it was the work of God and that Cennick would cease to be an effective preacher if he did not welcome such behaviour. In response Cennick walked alone in the woods at Kingswood and wept at what was happening until he felt God telling him to ignore John and follow the example of Charles.

Following Charles meant two things. First, Cennick deliberately either ignored those who shouted out or told them to shut up. As a consequence, he says 'all fits and crying ceased wherever I came, and a blessing attended my labours'.[26] Second, and in some ways this is even more interesting, Cennick refocused his preaching so that he dwelt less on Hell and much more on Christ's love and on God's readiness to forgive sinners. Presumably that must have reflected his experience of hearing Charles preach. It was, of course, a brave thing to do to oppose John, and Cennick writes that his discouragement of emotional behaviour 'opened a way for Mr Wesley and me to jar'.[27] It used to be commonly said that Charles was hostile to the decision to use lay helpers in preaching, but John Cennick's story runs counter to that. Charles was clearly hugely influential in developing the young layman's abilities – and not just in preaching, because at this time Charles was also acting as an editor of Cennick's first attempts at hymn writing.

In John's Journal account of his time in Bristol from 9–14 October and 20–31 October 1739, there is nothing about his exchanges with Cennick or any comment about what his brother had achieved, but there is a reference to him preaching twice on the subject of Christian perfection on Sunday 21 October. He says this was necessary to counter 'a slackness creeping in among them who had begun to run well'. Charles and Cennick both fully supported that it was right for a Christian to strive for perfection, but neither of them thought a state of perfection was attainable. John did. He preached again on 'the nature and extent of

Christian perfection' when he revisited Bristol in mid-November. It is fair to assume the theme of attaining perfection featured prominently in his subsequent four preaching visits to Bristol (from 9–31 January 1740, from 5 March to 6 April, from 12–20 April, and from 3 May to 2 June), because by the summer of 1740 there was a small but growing number of members at the New Room who were claiming they had attained Christian perfection. Cennick's unhappiness over such claims led to what might be termed a 'perfectionist crisis' in 1740 – one that was in its own way as destructive as the more famous perfectionist crisis of 1763.

If one looks at what had been achieved in just over a year not just in Bristol and Kingswood but also in London and elsewhere, it is easy to see why the revival movement had acquired the capacity for self-destruction. John and Charles fundamentally disagreed with Whitefield's Calvinist theology, and the Moravian leadership increasingly disliked the emotional behaviour encouraged by John and claimed the Wesleyan emphasis on striving to live a good Christian life was weakening the proclamation of salvation by faith. The tensions surfaced first in London and that is why Charles did not return to Bristol as quickly as originally envisaged. He spent not just the winter but almost the first six months of 1740 working in London. When Charles did return to Bristol on 21 June for a brief eight day visit, he was struck by its relative harmony. At the New Room he found 'peace, unity, and love', and he wrote of Kingswood: 'O what simplicity is in this childlike people! A spirit of contrition and love ran through them. Here the seed has fallen upon good ground . . . O that our London brethren would come to school to Kingswood! These are what they pretend to be.'[28] One event that particularly pleased him was being able to preach to a huge gathering of the colliers' children. Charles estimated that a thousand attended.

However, when Charles returned to Bristol on 9 July 1740 – and this time he stayed until the end of December – the seeds of dissension became apparent. For a start he had to lodge at the New Room because he and John were no longer welcome in the home of Whitefield's sister, Elizabeth. Indeed, she was shortly to start mounting a campaign in the New Room to have them excluded from preaching there because of their attacks on her brother's Calvinist thinking. This, of course, made Cennick's continued support all the more vital. Cennick was both a Calvinist and an admirer of the Moravians and he was a known disciple of Whitefield. No wonder Charles wrote in response to the 100 per cent public support he received from Cennick: 'Never did I find my spirit more knit to him.'[29] It

9

may well help explain why Charles made no objection to Cennick extending his role as a preacher way beyond Kingswood to a number of the villages in South Gloucestershire, including Upton Cheyney, Hanham, Downend, Hambrook, Bridgeyate, Siston, Westerleigh, Tockington and Elberton, and then into Wiltshire. The growing controversy in the region about the use of Cennick may have been a factor in why the vicar at the Temple Church, Henry Beacher, humiliated Charles on 27 July by denying him access to Holy Communion.

On 6 August 1740, Charles fell seriously ill and he was effectively out of action until mid-September. John Cennick then took over Charles's preaching appointments, including those at the New Room. He wrote to John Wesley in London: 'Pray for me that I may be humble [and] willing to be led by the Lord's hand whithersoever he pleaseth!'[30] Some people, of course, saw Cennick's preaching as inferior because he was not ordained. This kind of prejudice is evident in the following account written by Elizabeth Sayce, whose husband was a society member at the New Room:

> One night my husband and I were coming to the [New] Room where I expected to hear . . . [Mr Charles Wesley, but we were told] that Mr Cennick was to be there, at which I was so displeased that I would have returned [home] . . . had not my husband used his utmost persuasions that I might not. But as soon as I came to the [New] Room I was for going out.[31]

She stayed and she goes on to say that Cennick led the worship so well that she left rejoicing and shortly afterwards became a Methodist herself, joining one of the female bands.

Unfortunately, at the New Room Cennick increasingly found himself at odds with a Moravian called Edward Nowers, who had become the leader of those claiming they had attained perfection. He also found himself under attack from Whitefield's sister for his continued support for the Wesleys. Charles was to complain to George Whitefield about her actions when he recovered:

> Your sister (God help her, God convert her) is far, very far, from the kingdom of heaven . . . She is a snare and a stumbling block to many young persons who did run well. She miserably deceives her own soul, saying peace, peace, peace, when there is no peace . . . Infinite

Charles Wesley's role in the formative early years in Bristol

pains have been taken with her to set her against my brother and me. She hears railings against us from morning to night . . . [and] she has shown all envy, hatred, malice and revenge. She watches over the bands for evil and labours to bring all she can from our fellowship . . . I know not what to do with her, or for her . . . Many, I know, desire nothing so much as to see George Whitefield and John Wesley at the head of different parties, as is plain from their truly devilish plans to effect it.[32]

On 2 September 1740, John arrived in Bristol for a few days and he dealt with a court case which had arisen over mob attacks on society members. By that stage Charles was beginning to recover from what he had thought was going to be a terminal illness and he was attributing his survival to God. However, it was not until 18 September that Charles recovered sufficiently to preach at the New Room. He comments that he agreed he would do so for just fifteen minutes but God gave him the strength to do so for an hour and a half! Despite his frailty Charles helped avert a potential riot in Bristol that same month. An increase in the cost of bread had caused great hardship and a thousand colliers decided to march into the city in protest. Some of those who had attended Methodist meetings tried to argue against this, but they were intimidated into going along with it. According to Charles, they were told that they would be buried alive in their pits if they did not join in. Charles rode out to meet the advancing mob and urged them to return home. Those colliers who refused to listen to him began to attack those who were responsive to his words:

> I rode up to a ruffian who was striking one of our colliers, and prayed him rather to strike me. He would not, he said, for all the world, and was quite overcome. I turned upon one who had struck my horse, and he also sank like a lamb. Wherever I turned Satan lost ground.[33]

The outcome was that some colliers gained the courage to turn back while those who continued kept their protest peaceful. No stronger example could be given of both Charles's courage and of the influence now being exerted by Methodism.

That autumn, however, Cennick's loyalty was severely tested first by Charles and then by John. Charles's position on the Calvinist dispute confused and puzzled Cennick. Quite often Charles was actively communicating his friendship and love for Whitefield and Harris, and expressing his determination not to let theological differences break up their relationship, saying things like: 'I do not think the difference considerable. I shall never dispute with you . . . My soul is set upon peace.'[34] However, at the same time in his preaching he was constantly condemning Calvinist ideas and making reference to Whitefield's erroneous beliefs. And, of course, John Wesley was doing the same in London. As a consequence, first William Seward, who had helped fund the building of the New Room and Kingswood House, and then the Welsh evangelist Howell Harris, strongly urged Cennick to use his influence to make the Wesleys adopt a more conciliatory approach.

Cennick tried to persuade Charles to moderate his language but got nowhere. On 4 November 1740, faced with listening to yet another sermon in which Charles attacked the views of Whitefield, Cennick rebelled and for the first time refused to publicly endorse what was being said. Charles was flabbergasted but the issue was not resolved because he had to leave almost immediately afterwards for a preaching tour in Wales (ironically to work alongside the Calvinist Howell Harris). In Charles's absence John Wesley arrived in Bristol on 10 November. Cennick chose that moment to try and persuade him to denounce those claiming perfection. This seemed to him essential because Edward Nowers was publicly altering the words of the Lord's Prayer. He was saying 'Forgive *them* their trespasses. . .' to indicate that he was perfect and had no need to ask for forgiveness for himself.[35] Knowing that Nowers was one of John Wesley's favoured protégés, Cennick asked one of the leading female members at the New Room, Mrs Norman, to back him up. She agreed but that made no difference. John refused to listen to either of them and heavily criticised them for maligning Nowers. As far as John was concerned Nowers had every right to claim perfection:

> I see all his behaviour, and hear almost all his words . . . I am apt to think every day will give me fresh occasion to stand amazed at the goodness of God . . . [in] giving him to me. He was the man I wanted. I have not yet personally known any other who had so much gentleness and long-suffering toward them that are out of the way . . . I think him to be full of love and Christ and the Holy Ghost.[36]

There was, according to Cennick, a mighty row. In the wake of this a hugely disgruntled Cennick gave vent to his feelings to some of the colliers at Kingswood. The colliers felt that Cennick had been treated very badly but their anger could not be directed against John Wesley because he had left for London after the argument. As a consequence some of them heckled Charles when he preached to them on his return from Wales on 30 November. Knowing nothing of Cennick's row with his brother over the behaviour of Nowers, Charles understandably but wrongly assumed that the heckling stemmed entirely from Cennick's promotion of Calvinist thinking: 'The poison of Calvin has drunk up their spirit of love . . . Alas! We have set the wolf to keep the sheep! God give me great moderation toward him, who, for many months, has been undermining our doctrine and authority.'[37]

This error was almost certainly seized on by Edward Nowers and the perfectionists. Among their number was Thomas Maxfield, who perhaps saw in this his opportunity to replace Cennick as the favoured lay preacher in Bristol. The perfectionists began doing all they could to defame Cennick. A meeting between Charles and Cennick on 2 December failed to effect a reconciliation. There is perhaps a clue as to why it failed in the draft letter that Charles wrote afterwards to Cennick. In it he does refer briefly to his own annoyance at Cennick's refusal to back him up: 'God is my witness how condescendingly loving I have been toward you. Yet did you so forgot yourself as both openly and privately to contradict my doctrine'. But the bulk of the letter is about Cennick's treatment of John: 'You came to Kingswood upon my brother sending for you. You served under him in the gospel as a son. I need not say how well he loved you. You used the authority he gave you to overthrow his doctrine. You everywhere contradicted it. Whether true or false, is not the question.'[38]

Charles's unquestioning loyalty to John overrode any chance that Cennick might have had of being listened to at the meeting. But by rejecting Cennick, Charles knew he was endangering all that he and his brother had done. He wrote to John that in Kingswood 'they hold JC's leading-strings', and there was a danger 'not a man will stay with us by [the time of] your coming again.'[39] John thought Charles was over-reacting and told him not to send the letter he had written to Cennick. He returned to Bristol on 13 December to repair 'the breaches which had been made . . . [and] heal the jealousies and misunderstandings which had arisen.'[40] Space does not permit a detailed explanation of why John's intended reconciliation never took place, but a factor was undoubtedly that Charles was absent and once more in London. Had he been in

Bristol he might at the very least have confirmed that there was a genuine problem with the behaviour of Nowers and encouraged John to be cautious in accepting anything he or the other perfectionists said.

By Christmas, John was saying that he would preach at Kingswood rather than let Cennick do so. This backfired because only a handful of people turned up to hear Wesley because, as he wrote in his journal: 'My congregation was gone to hear Mr Cennick, so that (except for a few from Bristol) I had not above two or three men and as many women'.[41] By January 1741, John was trying in vain to persuade another of his helpers, Joseph Humphreys, to take Cennick's place, but Humphreys told him he could not happily 'do anything in opposition to Mr Cennick' and that Nowers was not to be trusted.[42] That same month a distraught Cennick chose to write to Whitefield asking him to return and take over the leadership:

> How glorious did the gospel seem once to flourish in Kingswood! I spake of the everlasting love of Christ with sweet power . . . But now bro. Charles is suffered to open his mouth against the truth, while the frighted sheep gaze and fly, as if no shepherd was among them . . . It is just as though Satan was now making war with the saints . . . With universal redemption bro. Charles pleases the world. Bro. John follows him in everything. I believe no atheist can more preach against predestination than they. And all who believe election are counted enemies to God, and called so. I am as [one] alone. I am in the midst of the plague . . . If God give thee leave, make haste.[43]

Somehow copies of that letter were handed out in London on 1 February 1741. This played beautifully into the hands of Cennick's enemies and, when John returned to Bristol, he expelled him from membership on 28 February, thus initiating a major split in the revival. The perfectionists had persuaded him that Cennick (amongst others) needed to be punished 'for talebearing, backbiting, and evil-speaking . . . for [their] dissembling, lying and slandering'.[44] Ironically, that same day Charles wrote from London warning John to be cautious about listening to whatever those claiming perfection might be saying: '[On the subject of perfection] you spoke not from your own experience, and those on whose experience you built your doctrine, are but of yesterday. None of them in Christianity longer than a few months – it does not yet appear what they shall be.'[45]

14

Within a few days of Cennick's expulsion about a third of the membership at Kingswood left and formed the nucleus of what became a new Calvinistic Methodist society. One collier later wrote: 'We were all attached to Cennick and looked on him as our minister.'[46] Membership at the New Room was also seriously affected. Whitefield arrived back from America in March. One of his first actions when he visited Bristol was to denounce the idea that anyone was perfect. Interestingly, there has survived a letter from Charles written two years later in June 1743 which could possibly be seen as a partial admission that he and John had not handled the issue of those claiming salvation and perfection well:

> We certainly have been too rash and easy in allowing persons for believers upon their own testimony, nay and even persuading them into a false opinion of themselves. Some souls it is doubtless necessary to encourage; but it should be done with prudence & caution . . . 'By their fruits ye shall know them.'[47]

Whitefield, Harris and Cennick were all keen to patch up the quarrel, but they faced pressure from their followers to defend Calvinism, and Whitefield therefore felt obliged to go into print and publish a defence of their theological position. This did not encourage either John or Charles to listen to their peace overtures. Charles returned to Bristol in early April. Although he was usually far more amenable than John, he was shaken by the impact of the disunity he saw in both Bristol and Kingswood, and it is worth reading his account of events on the weekend of 11–12 April 1741. First, he recounts how certain individuals who were dying declared the truth of what he had been preaching – that salvation was open to all. Next, he describes how their assurance of salvation led to other members at Kingswood experiencing the Holy Spirit. As a consequence, when the Calvinists returned from listening to Cennick, he says they were met with 'a flame of love' and that he then arranged for a communion service in Kingswood House:

> I had prayed God to show me some token if this was his will concerning us: and, indeed, my prayer was answered; for such a sacrament was I never present at before. We received the sure pledges of our Saviour's dying love, and were most of us filled with all peace and joy in believing.[48]

It seemed to Charles that God was telling him to stick firm to proclaiming that salvation was for all and not to water that message down by making concessions. Hence the anti-Calvinist hymns that he produced that summer.

The role of Charles as a pastor comes across very vividly in the journal entries written from April to August 1741: 'God every day adds fresh seals to my ministry'.[49] His effectiveness in that role, combined with his preaching talent and the absence of Whitefield from Bristol, enabled Charles slowly but surely to rebuild the numbers in attendance at the Wesleyan societies. According to Cennick, he and Charles tried to patch things up. Unfortunately, he does not provide the date of their meeting, only its outcome. He says he told Charles that he believed in a pre-ordained elect but also that the offer of salvation was for all and that Charles then lost his temper:

> At this he fell into a violent passion and affrighted all at table, and rising from the table, he said he would go directly and preach against me, and accordingly did . . . He called also Calvin the first-born son of the Devil, and set all his people into a bitter hatred of me and those who were with me.[50]

One can understand Charles's frustration at Cennick's theological naivety.

Charles's success in rebuilding the membership at both the New Room and Kingswood did not stop John Wesley making over forty visits to Kingswood in the year after Cennick's expulsion, so fearful was he of the possible collapse of his authority. A request from Whitefield for compensation for the money that he and his supporters had invested in the New Room and Kingswood House caused John to be particularly vitriolic. The Calvinistic Methodists had no option but to create what they hoped would be temporary new bases in Bristol and London – buildings that became known as Whitefield's Tabernacles. However, the focus of Whitefield, Harris and Cennick remained not on creating a rival organisation but on evangelical preaching. By October 1741, Whitefield was declaring: 'May all disputings cease, and each of us talk of nothing but Jesus and Him crucified! This is my resolution'.[51]

However, both the Wesleys knew that Whitefield could outshine them as a preacher and that he had the capacity to stamp Calvinist thinking on the revival. When huge crowds gathered to hear Whitefield in Bristol, Charles wrote a letter to his brother that John sensed was written in a panic. In it Charles said that they could not trust 'precious immortal souls . . . within the sound of predestination' and that they must therefore resist working with Whitefield until he had abandoned such thinking:

> [Mr Whitefield] preaches holiness very strongly and Free Grace to all, yet at the same time he uses expressions which necessarily imply Reprobation. He wraps it up in smoother language than before in order to convey the poison more successfully. Our society on this account go to hear him without any scruple or dread. We have seen the fatal effects of this devilish doctrine already, so that we cannot keep too great a distance from it. For my part, by the Grace of God, I never will be reconciled to reprobation, nor join with those who hold it. I wish that there might be a *real and thorough union* betwixt us . . . [but we must] regard not fair speeches.[52]

In practice, Charles was never as hardline as this letter might imply. For example, he was quick to go to the defence of John Cennick when a local magistrate chose to ignore mob attacks on Whitefield's Tabernacle. Charles said he found it hard to believe that a magistrate could turn a blind eye to such violence when it was known that Cennick was encouraging the colliers to become more law-abiding citizens:

> We work the works of God. . . [Those] who spent all their wages at the alehouse, now never go there at all, but keep their money to maintain their families; and have to give to those in want. Notorious swearers have now only the praises of God in their mouths. The good done among them is indisputable: our worst enemies cannot deny it.[53]

The real hardliner in practice was John Wesley, who repeatedly ensured that any unity talks with either the Calvinists or the Moravians failed. He refused to ever meet Cennick again and his hostility towards him was to endure even after Cennick's death. He famously wrote him off as 'that weak man'.[54]

Although both sides created more formal organisations in 1743 and 1744, there remained no desire on the Calvinistic side for a split and the growing persecution of all Methodists against the backdrop of the Jacobite Rebellion eventually forced both sides to work together. The friendship between Charles and George Whitefield soon resurfaced and became an important factor in the future success of Methodism. Indeed, for a few years Charles chose to work more closely with Whitefield and the Countess of Huntingdon than with his brother following the catastrophic clash of the brothers over John's wish to marry Grace Murray. By then, John Cennick, like Benjamin Ingham before him, had left Methodism to become a Moravian, but there is evidence that Charles still respected his work as a preacher. We know, for example, that Charles's wife went to hear Cennick preach and invited him to eat with her family, and that Charles tried to uphold the rights of Cennick's Moravian society against the machinations of the Methodists in Dublin.

Between 1739 and 1741 there is much to praise John Wesley for. Among other things, he admirably and courageously took on what George Whitefield had started and began transforming the way in which religious societies were organised. He commenced developing Methodism's first lay preachers, and he created the first two centres for the work of the revival at the New Room and Kingswood House. He also commenced the publishing that was to become a key factor in the growth of Methodism. However, I hope this short essay has shown that his contribution was not as one-sidedly wonderful as it has sometimes been portrayed. It was the preaching of George Whitefield, Charles Wesley and John Cennick that really established Methodism in Bristol and Kingswood, and a significant factor in Cennick's effectiveness as a preacher was that he modelled himself on Charles, who became his mentor.

Although John Wesley's own contribution as a preacher cannot be ignored, it should be more widely recognised that he sowed the seeds for three things that damaged the effectiveness of the revival: he promoted irrational behaviour, he encouraged people to claim that they were perfect, and he focused on the theological issues raised by Calvinism beyond what was necessary. Only on the latter issue does Charles also bear some of the blame. In later years, Whitefield's take on the division that took place in 1741 was a simple one: 'Busybodies on both sides blew up the coals. We harkened too much to tale bearers.'[55] It was a view that Charles also came to share:

> What dire device did the old serpent find
> to put asunder those whom God had joined?
> From folly and self-opinion rose,
> to sever friends who never yet were foes;
> to baffle and divert our noblest aim,
> confound our pride, and cover us with shame.[56]

Hence the fact that he later became a key upholder of working with Whitefield and other Calvinists even while continuing to proclaim loudly and clearly his own belief in salvation for all. Without the continued input from Whitefield and the other Calvinists that Charles encouraged, Wesleyan Methodism would not have grown in the way that it did.

Notes

1   Her account is one of six transcribed from testimonials collected by Charles Wesley in 1742 and printed in J. Barry and K. Morgan, *Reformation and Revival in Eighteenth-Century Bristol* (Bristol, 1994), p. 103.

2   John Cennick, 'Account of the Awakenings at Bristol and Kingswood, 1738, 1739', *Proceedings of the Wesley Historical Society* [henceforth *PWHS*], vol. 6, no. 6 (1908), 109.

3   George Whitefield, *Journals* (London, 1978); entry for 7 July 1739, p. 299.

4   Letter to John Wesley (25 June 1739) transcribed in Bicentennial Edition of *The Works of John Wesley*, general editors Frank Baker, Richard P. Heitzenrater, and Randy L. Maddox (Oxford, 1975–83, and Nashville TN, 1984–) [henceforth identified as *Works*, followed by volume and page numbers], *Works*, 25:661.

5   From manuscript in John Rylands Research Institute and Library as transcribed in F. Baker, 'John Wesley and Bishop Joseph Butler: A Fragment of John Wesley's Manuscript Journal, 16th to 24th August 1739', *PWHS*, vol. 42, no. 4 (1980), 93–100.

6   T. Jackson, *Journal of the Rev. Charles Wesley* (London, 1849) [henceforth *JCW*]; entry for 31 August 1739, pp. 166–7.

7   *JCW*; entry for 24 June 1739, p. 155.

8   *JCW*; entry for 1 September 1739, p. 167.

9   *JCW*; entry for 4 September 1739, p. 168.

10 *JCW*; entries as dated, pp. 169, 171, 174.

11 He refers in a letter to John Wesley in March 1740 to being distracted 'by an unusual unnecessary premeditating what to preach upon' (F. Baker, *Charles Wesley as Revealed by his Letters* [London, 1948], p. 38). He wrote in a later letter to Walter Shirley on 12 January 1760: 'I only plan out the heads and so trust the Lord for the rest' (John Rylands Research Institute and Library, DDPT 1/69).

12 Nelson's account as edited in J. Telford, *Wesley's Veterans, Vol III* (London, 1912), p. 65.

13 Valton's account edited in J. Telford, *Wesley's Veterans, Vol VI* (London, 1912), p. 19.

14 Cited in C. W. Flint, *Charles Wesley and his Colleagues* (Washington D.C., 1957), p. 148.

15 J. Whitehead, *The Life of the Rev John Wesley with the Life of the Rev Charles Wesley* (U.S. 1844 reprint of London 1793 edition), p. 210.

16 Barry and Morgan, *Reformation and Revival*, pp. 102–4.

17 John Rylands Research Institute and Library, Early Methodist Volume, MS dated 19 May 1740, available online at https://www.library.manchester.ac.uk/services/digitisation-services/projects/rapture-and-reason/ (accessed 23 October 2023).

18 *JCW*; entry for 3 September 1739, p. 167.

19 His account is transcribed in G. A. Nuttall, 'Charles Wesley in 1739. By Joseph Williams of Kidderminster', *PWHS*, vol. 42, no. 6 (1980), 181–5.

20 *JCW*; entry for 16 September 1739, pp. 173–4.

21 *JCW*; entry for 28 September 1739, p. 182.
22 *JCW*; entry as dated, p. 176.
23 *JCW*; entry as dated, p. 186.
24 *JCW*; entry as dated, pp. 186–7.
25 John Cennick, 'Account of the Awakenings at Bristol and Kingswood, 1738, 1739', *PWHS*, vol. 6, no. 6 (1908), 109.
26 Ibid.
27 Ibid.
28 *JCW*; entry for 22 June 1740, p. 242.
29 *JCW*; entry for 27 July 1740, p. 246.
30 John Rylands Research Institute and Library, Wesley College, Bristol archive (GB 1080 MSS), letter of 16 August 1740, General Antiquarian Collections D6/1/206.
31 Letter to Charles transcribed in Barry and Morgan, *Reformation and Revival*, 96.
32 John Rylands Research Institute and Library, letter of 1 September 1740, DDCW 6/34.
33 *JCW*; entry for 22 September 1740, p. 249.
34 John Rylands Research Institute and Library, letter to George Whitefield (1 September 1740), DDCW 6/34.
35 John Cennick, 'Account of the Awakenings at Bristol and Kingswood, 1738, 1739', *PWHS*, vol. 6, no. 8 (1908), 134.
36 Letter from John Wesley to James Hutton (21 March 1740), *Works*, 26:9–10.
37 *JCW*; entry for 30 November 1740, pp. 262–3.
38 T. Jackson, *The Life of the Rev. Charles Wesley*, vol. 1 (London, 1841), pp. 250–1.
39 Letter to John Wesley (3 December 1740), K. G. C. Newport and G. Lloyd (eds), *The Letters of Charles Wesley, vol. I, 1728–56* (Oxford, 2013), p. 91.
40 Journal entries for 14 and 15 December 1740 in *Works*, 19:174.
41 Ibid., entry for 26 December 1740, p. 175.
42 L. Tyerman, *Life and Times of John Wesley*, vol. 1 (London, 1856), p. 347.
43 Letter dated 17 January 1741 in *Works*, 19:183. Recorded as journal entry for 22 February 1741.
44 Ibid., entry for 28 February 1741, p. 184.
45 Wesley's Chapel, London, letter of 28 February 1741, Dodsworth Bequest LGWMM 2001/8281/2.
46 Testimonial of Samuel Tippett transcribed in Barry and Morgan, *Reformation and Revival*, p. 124.
47 Letter dated 13 June 1743 and known to have been addressed to 'a son of the gospel'. Newport and Lloyd, vol. I, p. 106.
48 *JCW*; entry for 12 April 1741, p. 267.
49 *JCW*; entry for 26 April 1741, p. 270.
50 *The Moravian Messenger*, vol. XVI.
51 Jackson, *Life of Charles Wesley*, pp. 266–7.
52 John Rylands Research Centre and Library, letter to John Wesley (28 September 1741), DDCW 1/13.
53 *JCW*; entry for 22 September 1741, p. 249.
54 Journal entry for 12 October 1760, *Works*, 21:283.
55 Jackson, *Life of Charles Wesley*, p. 260.
56 'An Epistle to the Rev George Whitefield' in George Osborn, *The Poetical Works of John and Charles Wesley*, vol. 6 (London, 1869), p. 287.

SONGS OF RENEWAL: THE LANGUAGE OF RENEWAL IN THE HYMNS OF CHARLES WESLEY

Paul W. Chilcote

This essay discusses Charles Wesley as hymnwriter, focusing on his use of the terms 'restore', 'renew' and 'revive' in the Wesleys' 1780 Collection of Hymns. Each of these core concepts is itself developed extensively in Charles's corpus. Thus 'restoration' appears in terms of the restoration of the sinner's heart to wholeness, the reinstatement of the image of God in the believer, and the display of Christ-like love in the believer's life. But Charles had a wider vision, of the establishment of God's kingdom on earth, one of justice and peace. He also eagerly anticipates the New Heaven and New Earth which would be inaugurated by the Second Coming of Jesus Christ. Finally, Charles's concept of 'revival' places a clear responsibility upon the church, and specifically on Methodists. He urges his hearers to participate in a revival which encompasses their own behaviour, peace and justice in the wider world, and ultimately the renewal of all creation.

Keywords: Charles Wesley, hymns, Methodism, revival, theology

Restoration implies something lost and something found. The terms renewal, retrieval, recovery, and revival all point in the same direction: to be new again, to find again, to get again, to have life again. In talking with a craftsman who restores vintage cars one day, I learned that restoration means more than just making a vehicle's exterior look nice. A full restoration involves replacing nearly every part on the car with a newer, better working one, from the gauges on the dashboard to the lining of the boot's walls. Such restoration entails a lengthy, painstaking, and often complex process. To restore literally means to build up again and this was

https://doi.org/10.16922/jrhlc.10.2.3

the primary impetus behind the Wesleyan revival that arose within the Church of England during the eighteenth century. The Wesley brothers spearheaded a movement of spiritual renewal aimed at building up the church for the work of God's mission in the world.[1] The purpose of this essay is to examine the language of renewal in the hymns of Charles Wesley and to identify the salient elements of restoration, recovery, and renewal in his lyrical theology.

The language of renewal

An exhaustive analysis of Charles Wesley's own 'concept of renewal' here is hardly thinkable. So I am imposing two rather serious limits to the linguistic analysis of this study. First, I examine Charles's use of terms such as renew, restore, and revive (and their derivatives or cognates) in order to glean a road map for a larger exploration of his concept of renewal.

Secondly, I restrict myself to one primary, albeit pervasively influential source, namely, the 1780 *Collection of Hymns for the Use of the People Called Methodists*.[2] This *Collection* constitutes a body of lyrical material well-known and formational within the life of the movement; the hymns included in this *Collection* shaped the definition and ethos of the Methodist people, perhaps, more than any other. While I fully recognize the limitations and dangers of this design, I am also convinced of its benefits, and the portrait of renewal that emerges is both authentic and compelling.

A detailed examination of the *Collection* as a whole reveals some interesting facts which lead to several broad but significant generalizations related to the concept of restoration. The verb 'to renew' (in the form renew[s] and renewed), appears thirty-four times in the hymns of the *Collection*.[3] Wesley uses the language of renewal primarily with regards to the change of one's heart (six instances) and the restoration of love (six instances). These two categories dominate this particular set of hymns, especially when hymns that reference similar concepts, such as the renewal of the mind, spirit, soul, or self (corollary to the heart) and hymns that emphasize the recovery of holiness and the image of Christ (corollary to love), are included. Taken together, these two categories constitute two-thirds of these hymns. In addition to this, Charles also prays for the renewal of strength, vigour, or labour (six hymns) and emphasizes God's work in the more cosmic dimensions of renewal. But these hymns demonstrate that Wesley conceives renewal primarily in terms of a personal, interior, and spiritual change.

Charles's preferred terminology with regards to renewal, however, revolves around the concept of 'restoration' (seventy-seven instances of restore[s], restored, Restorer, unrestored, and All-restoring in sixty-one hymns).[4] Here again, the two categories previously discussed are preponderant. The interior restoration of love, holiness, perfection, purity, or the image of God are referred to in fifteen hymns. The restoration of the soul, spirit, or self are described in thirteen hymns. Most of the remaining hymns elevate the personal dimension of God's restorative work as well – the recovery of life, peace, health, and most importantly, paradise or heaven (seven hymns). Wesley identifies the source of restoration in seven hymns, celebrating the fact that we are restored by grace, by Jesus or Jesus's blood, and by the action of God – the 'All-restoring'. Only three hymns refer to the restoration of God's kingdom, the universal restorative work of God in nature, and the eschatological consummation of all things in Christ. Interestingly, nearly half these hymns are couched in the past tense – 'restored' – with the implication that the renewal is an accomplished fact. While Charles affirms an eschatological 'not yet' with regards to the restorative work of the Triune God, he also alludes to the present reality of restoration, a dimension of God's work to be celebrated. Wesley casts almost all his uses of the term 'restore' in the form of prayer, as in 'Thine image to my soul restore'.[5] In these hymns the singer yearns for restoration and reaches out toward it in hope with great expectation.[6]

In a number of these hymns Wesley enhances this 'language of renewal' with compounded or multiple uses of these terms. Several selections from a dozen such hymns suffice to illustrate Charles's exploitation of the images through this device.[7] In his lyrical paraphrase of the Aaronic blessing (Numbers 6:24–6), he prays:

> Come, Father, Son, and Holy-Ghost,
> One God in Persons Three,
> Bring back the heavenly blessing, lost
> By all mankind, and me:
>
> Thy favour, and thy nature too,
> To me, to all restore;
> Forgive, and after God renew,
> And keep us evermore.[8]

Throughout his literary corpus, Charles employs a unique expression to define the outcome of God's restorative process. He describes the fully restored disciple as a transcript of the Trinity, one of his most poignant metaphors. Without using that specific language, one of his hymns on the Trinity articulates this portrait of the redeemed child of God:

> Thy powerful, wise, and loving mind
>   Did our creation plan,
> And all the glorious Persons join'd
>   To form thy fav'rite, man.
>
> Again thou didst, in council met,
>   Thy ruin'd work restore,
> Establish'd in our first estate,
>   To forfeit it no more:
>
> And when we rise in love renew'd,
>   Our souls resemble thee,
> An image of the Tri-une God
>   To all eternity.[9]

Two couplets from another Trinity hymn succinctly reiterate this salient conception of restoration:

> Restorer of thine image lost,
>   Thy various offices make known;
>
> O that we now in love renew'd,
>   Might blameless in thy sight appear.[10]

In a composite lyrical exposition of Psalm 130:8 and Jeremiah 4:1, Wesley tersely describes the holistic consequences of spiritual renewal, implied in the supplication of the child of God: 'My fallen nature renew' and 'Thy kingdom now restore'![11] This conjunction of personal and cosmic dimensions of renewal pervades Wesley's thinking, as we shall see. In a hymn 'For Children' he weaves together the language of recovery, restoration, and renewal in this moving prayer:

Answer on them the end of all
  Our cares, and pains, and studies here,
On them, recover'd from their fall,
  Stampt with the humble character,
Rais'd by the nurture of the Lord,
To all their paradise restor'd.

Error and ignorance remove,
  Their blindness both of heart and mind,
Give them the wisdom from above,
  Spotless, and peaceable, and kind,
In knowledge pure their minds renew,
And store with thoughts divinely true.[12]

In just over 100 hymns of the *Collection* (about one out of five hymns), Wesley uses forms of the verbs renew, restore, and revive. The location of these hymns in the volume reveals some interesting facts. First, these hymns appear in every section of the *Collection* except one – 'Describing Hell' (perhaps no surprises here). This fact, at the very least, demonstrates the pervasiveness of these themes. Half the hymns, however, appear in just five of the twenty-nine sections. Sixteen hymns are found in 'Part IV. Section VII. For believers groaning for full redemption', and thirteen are drawn from 'Part IV. Section I. For believers rejoicing'. These constitute nearly a third of the hymns related to renewal. Fourteen hymns come from two sections (seven hymns each), both of which focus on the process of being 'brought to birth'. The remaining seven hymns relate to the intercessory ministry of the believer.

It is somewhat dangerous to draw anything but very broad generalizations from this kind of analysis, but two conclusions can be made boldly and without qualification. First, the theme of restoration or renewal pervades this *Collection*. For comparative purposes, a parallel analysis of the term 'faith', which could easily be argued the most central theme of the Wesleyan revival, appears in 120 hymns in this corpus, not that much more in number than the set of hymns we have been exploring here. Secondly, these hymns that allude to restoration and renewal focus the singer on the goal of the fullest possible restoration and the joy that accompanies it. While this is primarily personal and interior, it is not exclusively so.

These are some of the conclusions we can draw from this raw data, the minute detail, related to the language of renewal in the *Collection*. Of greater significance, however, are the major themes that revolve around these images. Three particular themes – distinct but inseparable from one another – characterize Wesley's concept of renewal: the restoration of perfect love in the child of God, the recovery of God's rule, and the revival of the church as God's instrument of renewal in the world.

'To perfect love restored'

In several selections from *Hymns and Sacred Poems* (1742), Wesley describes the condition of 'a poor sinner'. The heading for his lyrical paraphrase of Revelation 3:17 simply replicates the verse: 'Wretched, and miserable, and poor, and blind, and naked'. In order to properly envisage the goal toward which restoration moves, one must consider humanity's loss and the plight of the human condition. The opening stanzas of this hymn describe the fallen state of humanity in graphic terms and conclude that humanity 'gasps to be made whole'. In the face of human desperation, Charles offers this vision of renewal in love:

> In the wilderness I stray,
> My foolish heart is blind,
> Nothing do I know; the way
> Of peace I cannot find;
> Jesu, Lord, restore my sight,
> And take, O take the veil away,
> Turn my darkness into light,
> My midnight into day.
>
> Naked of thine image, Lord,
> Forsaken, and alone,
> Unrenew'd, and unrestor'd
> I have not thee put on:
> Over me thy mantle spread,
> Send down thy likeness from above,
> Let thy goodness be display'd,
> And wrap me in thy love.

> Jesu, full of truth and grace,
>   In thee is all I want:
> Be the wanderer's resting-place,
>   A cordial to the faint;
> Make me rich, for I am poor,
> In thee may I my Eden find,
>   To the dying health restore,
>   And eye-sight to the blind.
>
> Cloath me with thy holiness,
>   Thy meek humility,
> Put on me thy glorious dress,
>   Endue my soul with thee;
> Let thy image be restor'd,
> Thy name, and nature let me prove,
>   With thy fulness fill me, Lord,
>   And perfect me in love.[13]

Unrenewed and unrestored, those who are blind and lost in the wilderness seek wholeness. First, God restores sight. Next, God offers companionship for a journey leading back to Eden – a process that restores health. The ultimate goal is the restoration of the image of God which solicits the supplication of the singer, 'With thy fullness fill me, Lord, / And perfect me in love'. This hymn essentially explicates the *via salutis* as a process of restoration. Wesley conflates this pathway toward wholeness into the four lines of a hymn based on Matthew 14:36:

> Come, Saviour, come, and make me whole,
>   Intirely all my sins remove,
> To perfect health restore my soul,
>   To perfect holiness and love.[14]

This theme of 'love restored' dominates the lyrical theology of Charles Wesley. He views this as God's most treasured promise. In a lyrical paraphrase of Micah 7:20 he enunciates this first element in his concept of renewal:

> Let us to perfect love restor'd
>   Thine image here retrieve,

And in the presence of our Lord
The life of angels live.[15]

I have no need to fully explicate this central Wesleyan theme (of both brothers) as it has been explored in great detail.[16] Several important observations about this aspect of restoration are germane, however, and well-illustrated with hymns from the *Collection*.

The restoration of the heart

One of Wesley's more famous hymns which appeared in a number of collections, including that of 1780, expresses his most mature vision of a life restored to perfect holiness or love:

O for a heart to praise my God,
A heart from sin set free!
A heart that always feels thy blood,
So freely spilt for me!

A heart in every thought renewed
And full of love divine,
Perfect and right and pure and good,
A copy, Lord, of thine.

Thy nature, gracious Lord, impart;
Come quickly from above;
Write thy new name upon my heart,
Thy new, best name of Love.[17]

Given the fact that whatever is written on the heart reflects the true character of the person, God must restore, or transcribe, the heart fully. This hymn celebrates the heart of the believer – the heart upon which God has written the law of love. God writes on the heart, shapes the character, forms the disciple – restores the image of Christ in the child. In a hymn most likely written for Elizabeth Carr, whom Wesley baptized in the river at Cowley near Oxford in 1748, he prays:

Father, all thy love reveal,
Jesus all thy mind impart,
Holy Ghost, renew, and dwell
Forever in her heart.[18]

The restoration of the image of Christ

In a hymn from the section of the *Collection* related to 'groaning for full redemption', Charles appeals to the Trinity to bring this great work to completion:

> Father, Son, and Holy-Ghost,
>   In council join again
> To restore thine image, lost
>   By frail apostate man:
> O might I thy form express,
>   Thro' faith begotten from above,
> Stampt with real holiness,
>   And fill'd with perfect love![19]

These images actually pervade this section of the hymnal as Charles explores the many dimensions of redemption's goal. He concludes a twenty-stanza reflection on 'the mind of Christ', based upon Philippians 2:5, with this confident affirmation:

> I shall fully be restor'd
> To the image of my Lord,
> Witnessing to all mankind,
> Jesu's is a PERFECT mind.[20]

The phrase 'restoration of the image of Christ', the positive expression of his 'renewal of our fallen nature', reflects the heart of Wesley's vision of 'the one thing needful'.[21]

The restoration of Christ-like love

Restoration of the image of Christ implies Christ-likeness.[22] In a hymn which he located in the section on 'full redemption' for the two volume *Hymns and Sacred Poems* published in 1749, Wesley explicitly connects this restoration with conformity to Christ:

> We rest on His word.
> We shall here be restored
> To His image; the servant shall be as his Lord.[23]

Those who bear the image of Christ conform to him in mind and life, and more than anything else, this infers Christ-like love. The 'believer brought to the birth' cries out: 'O cut short the work, and make / Me now a creature new! . . . Let my life declare thy power; / To thy perfect love restored'.[24] Hymns in the 'believers rejoicing' section of the *Collection* are replete with references to 'love renewed', several of them drawn from the Trinity hymns. 'O that we now in love renew'd / Might blameless in thy sight appear'.[25] Another from this collection echoes themes already explored:

> And when we rise in love renew'd,
>   Our souls resemble thee,
> An image of the Tri-une God
>   To all eternity.[26]

As one hymn explaining the purpose of life puts it so succinctly: '[We] rise renewed in perfect love'.[27]

This personal, spiritual restoration of love divine in the heart of the believer is so central and so pervasive that there is a sense in which all other aspects of renewal occupy a space secondary to this. But this is not fully true; this only reflects part of the story of God's work of restoration. The spiritual renewal of the person from the inside out – this heart work – leads, or should lead, to robust engagement in God's rule and reign in the world. The defining elements of Jesus's life and ministry revolved around the kingdom of God – preached and lived. In this gospel, personal salvation was only the opening act, so to speak, of the much larger drama of redemption. God makes a way possible for the recovery of a partnership abandoned by God's children, therefore, if those children are to live out their lives – their vocation – with integrity in the world.

'Thy kingdom now restore'

Perry Shaw, a noted theological educator and proponent of integrated, missional models of education, identifies the core aspects of God's continuing work into which we are all invited:

> The mission of God is the starting point of our identity and calling. The important thing is not what we are doing but what God is doing

in this world. God's creative and redemptive agenda is the consummate restoration of the good. In the revelation of his divine Triune character of love and holiness, and in as much as we are attuned to his nature, we are able to discover our true identity. God entrusts us to partner with him in the accomplishment of his mission – the extension of his shalom Kingdom.[28]

'Perfect love restored' not only entails the transformation of individual persons and their reconciliation with God through Christ in the power of the Spirit, it also involves the whole community of faith living into this larger redemptive narrative in partnership with God. Charles, like his brother, opposed any truncation of the gospel that failed to acknowledge this parallel calling – the proclamation and performance of God's *shalom* in an unjust and discordant world.

While he seldom employed language typically used today with regard to this aspect of renewal – this engagement in the reign of God—his hymns address a wide range of concerns related to God's kingdom.[29] Acts of justice and compassion vanquish evil and despair in God's economy, and Charles calls for those in the community of faith to practice them perennially in their commitment to God's rule.

Various forms of injustice and circumstances of despair clamoured for attention in Wesley's day, in particular, hunger, poverty, slavery, and war. As one might well expect, several hymns from the section of the *Collection* entitled 'For Believers Interceding for the World' address this issue, but none more potently than Charles's lyrical paraphrase of Isaiah's vision of the peaceable kingdom (11:6–7):

> Prince of universal peace,
> > Destroy the enmity,
> Bid our jars and discords cease,
> > Unite us all in thee.
> Cruel as wild beasts we are,
> 'Till vanquished by thy mercy's power,
> > We, like wolves, each other tear,
> > And their own flesh devour.
>
> But if thou pronounce the word
> > That forms our souls again,
> Love and harmony restored

> Throughout the earth shall reign;
>   When thy wondrous love they feel,
> The human savages are tame,
>   Ravenous wolves, and leopards dwell
>   And stable with the lamb.[30]

Likewise, Wesley produced an amazing body of hymnody related to the poor, calling forth the compassion of all within the family of Jesus.[31] Just one example from the *Collection* must suffice here – Charles's reflections on James 1:27:

> Thy mind throughout my life be shewn,
>   While listening to the wretch's cry,
> The widow's and the orphan's groan,
>   On mercy's wings I swiftly fly,
>   The poor and helpless to relieve,
>   My life, my all, for them to give.[32]

An affective experience of God's rule in one's heart and an outward performance of the kingdom through works of justice and compassion defined Wesley's vision of *shalom*, and he considered both dimensions to be essential to the recovery of peace and harmony in the world.

A hymn written by Henry More, a seventeenth-century Cambridge Platonist, and adapted by John Wesley, was most likely included among the intercessory hymns of the *Collection* because of its focus on the recovery of God's rule in this world:

> On all the earth thy Spirit shower;
>   The earth in righteousness renew;
> Thy kingdom come, and hell's o'erpower,
>   And to thy sceptre all subdue.[33]

Charles declares his trust and hope in God's promise in a stellar hymn on the Incarnation:

> All glory to God in the sky,
>   And peace upon earth be restor'd!
> O Jesus, exalted on high,
>   Appear our omnipotent Lord:

> Who meanly in Bethlehem born,
>   Didst stoop to redeem a lost race,
> Once more to thy creature return,
>   And reign in thy kingdom of grace.[34]

But there is an eschatological dimension of this kingdom work, as well, and Wesley's vision of God's rule extended far beyond this earthly realm.

God's restoration extends, in fact, to the entire cosmos, a concept Charles links with the image of new creation in 2 Corinthians 5:17. On 1 November 1755 a devastating earthquake hit Portugal, and the shock waves quickly spread, both literally and figuratively, across Europe. Once word of this tragedy reached Britain, King George II declared 6 February 1756 a day of fasting and prayer. Early in the new year, Charles published a set of seventeen hymns designed for use on this day.[35] He published two of these hymns which enunciate an apocalyptic theme in the section describing judgment in the *Collection*:

> Every fresh alarming token
>   More confirms thy faithful word,
> Nature (for its Lord hath spoken)
>   Must be suddenly restor'd:
> From this national confusion,
>   From this ruin'd earth and skies,
> See the times of restitution,
>   See the new creation rise![36]

In the second hymn Charles anticipates the joy of those who have aligned themselves with the purposes of God on the day of the Lord. The partner of God

> Sees this universe renew'd,
> The grand millennial reign begun,
>   Shouts with all the sons of God
>   Around th' eternal throne.

> Resting in this glorious hope
>   To be at last restor'd
> Yield we now our bodies up
> To earthquake, plague, or sword.[37]

One of Wesley's hymns entitled 'At the Parting of Friends', and included in the final section of the *Collection*, reflects the apex of his lyrical account of the consummation. This hymn is replete with the language of restoration and renewal:

> These eyes shall see them fall,
>   Mountains, and stars, and skies,
> These eyes shall see them all
>   Out of their ashes rise;
> These lips his praises shall rehearse,
> Whose nod restores the universe.
>
> According to his word,
>   His oath to sinners given,
> We look to see restor'd
>   The ruin'd earth and heaven,
> In a new world his truth to prove,
> A world of righteousness and love.
>
> Then let us wait the sound
>   That shall our souls release,
> And labour to be found
>   Of him in spotless peace,
> In perfect holiness renew'd,
> Adorn'd with Christ and meet for God.[38]

'Build up Thy rising church'

Wesley could not conceive any form of restoration outside the framework of the church – the community of God's faithful people.

> Now, Jesus, now thy love impart,
> To govern each devoted heart,
>   And fit us for thy will:
> Deep founded in the truth of grace,
> Build up thy rising church, and place
>   The city on the hill.[39]

Embracing God's gift of faith which leads to holiness of heart and engaging in partnership with God in the realization of *shalom* – holiness of life – only become real as these practices are lived out in community and in the concrete realities of life. While Wesley clearly affirmed that God's nod can, in and of itself, restore an entire universe, he also believed that God chose to include the church in this work – 'to serve the present age'.[40] While God will most certainly bring all things to completion in the end, the present affords the church ample opportunity to reflect God's work of restoration now. Moreover, the success of the church in this vocation depends, in large measure, on its ability to diagnose the condition of the church and to reclaim its true calling in the mission of God. Wesley's desire to revive primitive Christianity and to reclaim a missional vision of the church emanate from these concerns.

Primitive Christianity

Charles, like his brother, came to the conclusion that their beloved Church of England had abandoned its first love. They contended that circumstances coalesced in a way that compromised the spiritual vitality of the church. Their vision was truly 'ancient future', more concerned about a way forward filled with hope than a critique of the church's malaise or faithlessness, and they drew their vision from the earliest Christian communities of the New Testament. While the church, in some measure, retained the form of the primitive faith – something that lay dormant in its statements of faith and neglected practices of worship and discipleship – it had lost the power of godliness. In the face of this challenge, the Wesleys raised up a movement of renewal with the intention of rediscovering Christian authenticity.[41]

In 1743, at the outset of this revival, John Wesley published *An Earnest Appeal to Men of Reason and Religion* to defend the Methodist movement against the claim that he and his brother were attempting to undermine the established Church. In his second edition of this tract he appended a poem of his brother entitled 'Primitive Christianity'. In this lengthy composition Charles articulated the ideal of Christian faith and practice that the Methodists were trying to emulate and restore. This poem functions as a manifesto of renewal for the movement, structured in large measure on the outline of 1 Peter 2, and parallel in thought and aspiration to John's *The Character of a Methodist*.[42]

The poem – Hymns 16 and 17 of the *Collection* – is presented there in its original two segment division, Part I in fourteen and Part II in sixteen stanzas.[43] The opening line, 'Happy the souls that first believed' establishes primitive Christianity as the ideal and pattern for Charles's (and John's) reparative mission. 'Still let us in thy Spirit live', he sings, 'And to thy church the pattern give'.[44] Elsewhere he moves beyond aspiration to prescription with regard to this pattern and identifies some of its constitutive elements:

> Let us each for other care,
> Each his brother's burthen bear,
> To thy church the pattern give,
> Shew how true believers live.
>
> Free from anger, and from pride,
> Let us thus in God abide,
> All the depth of love express,
> All the height of holiness.[45]

Reflecting nostalgically on the 'golden days' of Jesus's first followers in the primitive church, he simply asks, 'Where shall I wander now to find / The successors they left behind?' (lines 17–18) and then demands, 'show me where the Christians live' (line 24).[46]

He contrasts 'a pure, believing multitude' (line 10) – his definition for the authentic community of faith – with 'different sects' (line 21) which peddle a false gospel devoid of the 'genuine mark of love' (line 26). Charles celebrates the signs of God's re-edifying presence (rebuilding the community of faith) among the Methodist people and endorses a classical vision of *ecclesia semper reformanda*.[47] While little direct critique of the Church of England will be found in this poem – Charles was a consummate son of the Church – in other hymns of the *Collection* he points to the pressing need of reform. The church's heart, he claims, like the heart of every individual, must be transformed. 'To all thy church and me', he pleads, 'Give a new, believing heart / That knows and cleaves to thee'.[48] 'Fill our church with righteousness', he prays, 'Our want of faith supply'.[49] A healthy church is a faithful church. But Charles knew his own church well enough to know that its deficiencies were not limited to benign neglect or spiritual amnesia; there were also forces within the church that were antithetical, in his view, to God's mission in the world.

Like his Puritan forebears, he yearned for the church to be a pure as well as a faithful community of God's people.

He exposed hypocrisy and corruption in the church, therefore, and applied a more radical prescription in hopes of recovery. Reflecting on the image of the church as the temple, as described in Jeremiah 7, he unleashed one of his most scathing criticisms of leaders within the church whose attitudes and actions were antithetical to the gospel:

> The men who slight thy faithful word
> In their own lies confide,
> These are the temple of the Lord,
> And heathens all beside!
> The temple of the Lord are these,
> The only church and true,
> Who live in pomp, and wealth, and ease,
> And Jesus never knew.
>
> The temple of the Lord – they pull
> Thy living temples down,
> And cast out every gracious soul
> That trembles at thy frown:
> The church – they from their pale expel
> Whom thou hast here forgiven:
> And all the synagogue of hell
> Are the sole heirs of heaven![50]

Despite malaise and disease in the church, Charles believed that a faithful remnant could always be found. Even among dry bones, the Spirit was at work to raise up authentic followers of Jesus 'to spread / The dead-reviving news'.[51] God would send this 'chosen band' through every nation, leaving no one behind, and restoring everyone who responded in faith to their 'first estate'.[52] Charles believed that God was restoring the church through the people called Methodists and that they were 'Raised by the breath of love divine'. 'We urge our way with strength renew'd', he claimed, 'The church of the first-born to join'.[53]

Missional vision

Charles and his brother rediscovered a 'mission-church paradigm' in their own day.[54] As I have written elsewhere:

> They believed that God designed the church as a redemptive community, a family that lives in and for God's vision of shalom in the world. God calls the church to bear witness to this dominion in every aspect of life. The church in this biblical paradigm draws committed Christian disciples perennially to Jesus and to one another in community for the purpose of spinning them out into the world in mission and service.[55]

The singular goal of this church-as-mission, in Wesley's understanding, is to partner with God in the restoration of perfect love, in all its dimensions, in the life of the world. Faithfulness in this adventure, which is both task and gift, entails an all-encompassing engagement of the disciple in God's reign. The difficult work of restoration claims of each disciple, 'All I have and all I am.'[56] Charles Wesley invites every child of God into the grand narrative of God's restoring work in which the blind are restored, the deaf hear his voice, and the lepers are cleansed – in which God makes all things new and establishes the rule of *shalom*. Moreover, he invites the community of faith to celebrate the God 'Who now is reviving His work in our days.'[57]

Notes

[1] The Wesleyan tradition as a movement of renewal in the church continues to invite thoughtful studies. See, P. W. Chilcote (ed.), *The Wesleyan Tradition: A Paradigm for Renewal* (Nashville TN, 2002); cf. H. Snyder, *Signs of the Spirit: How God Reshapes the Church* (Grand Rapids MI, 1989) and his earlier work, *The Radical Wesley and Patterns of Church Renewal* (Grand Rapids MI, 1987). With regards to the theological underpinnings of the Wesleyan paradigm of renewal, see, Chilcote, *Recapturing the Wesleys' Vision: An Introduction to the Faith of John and Charles Wesley* (Downers Grove IL, 2004) and Chilcote, *A Faith That Sings: Biblical Themes in the Lyrical Theology of Charles Wesley* (Eugene OR, 2016).

[2] Bicentennial Edition of *The Works of John Wesley*, general editors Frank Baker, Richard P. Heitzenrater, and Randy L. Maddox (Oxford, 1975–83, and Nashville, 1984–) [henceforth identified as *Works*, followed by volume and page numbers], *Works*, 7. Hymn texts presented here are those which appeared in the first edition of the original source; all bibliographical references refer both to the original location of the hymn and the location of the text in the *Collection*. I have used 'Charles Wesley's Published Verse',

Duke Center for Studies in the Wesleyan Tradition website, prepared and introduced by Randy L. Maddox, with the assistance of Aileen F. Maddox, with thanks for this amazing resource: https://divinity.duke.edu/initiatives/cswt/charles-published-verse (accessed 27 October 2023).

[3] *Works*, 7, Hymns 60, 69, 89, 105, 118, 138, 152, 227, 243, 248, 253, 286, 292, 294, 312, 314, 331, 334, 343, 346, 351, 362, 389, 398, 404, 445, 461, 465, 467, 479, 496, and 522.

[4] *Works*, 7, Hymns 9, 38, 56, 59, 60, 63, 72, 87, 95, 98, 103, 105, 106, 119, 129, 159, 163, 164, 166, 167, 172, 173, 179, 199, 203, 211, 219, 243, 248, 253, 266, 282, 321, 333, 345, 346, 353, 357, 358, 364, 374, 378, 383, 385, 390, 396, 398, 414, 420, 435, 440, 449, 461, 468, 498, 510, 511, 514, 519, 520, and 522.

[5] C. Wesley, *Hymns and Sacred Poems* (Bristol, 1742), p. 68, stanza 6; hereinafter *HSP* (1742); cf. *Works*, 7, Hymn 106:6.

[6] Allusions to 'revival', 'retrieval', and 'recovery' lead to the same conclusions. In addition to the simple affirmation of the process being God's work (four hymns), Charles's use of the term 'revive' (eleven hymns) connotes new life or resurrection for the believer more than any other emphasis. See *Works*, 7, Hymns 38, 44, 57, 159, 210, 243, 368, 424, 440, 477, and 505. He provides a panoply of images associated with the concept of 'retrieval' (twelve hymns). See *Works*, 7, Hymns 3, 6, 32, 89, 166, 192, 198, 261, 333, 346, 449, and 515. God retrieves us in the sense of saving us from sin, ruin, the loss of Eden, hell, the Tempter's power, and Satan's hands; positively, God retrieves for us our souls, his favour, his love, and preponderantly (three hymns), his image. Texts related to 'recovery' (just four hymns including the terms 'recover' and 'recovered') focus on peace, love, and purity – finding one's way home. See *Works*, 7, Hymns 71, 167, 360, and 461.

[7] See *Works*, 7, Hymns 38, 60, 105, 159, 243, 248, 253, 346, 398, 440, 461, and 522.

[8] C. Wesley, *Short Hymns on Select Passages of the Holy Scriptures*, 2 vols. (Bristol, 1762), 1:60, Hymn 200, hereinafter *Scripture Hymns*; cf. *Works*, 7, Hymn 243:1–2. Emphasis added.

[9] C. Wesley, *Hymns on the Trinity* (Bristol, 1767), p. 58, Hymn 87:2–3; hereinafter *Trinity Hymns*; cf. *Works*, 7, Hymn 248:46. Emphasis added.

[10] *Trinity Hymns*, pp. 98–9, Hymn 14:1 and 4; *Works*, 7, Hymn 253:1 and 4. Emphasis added.

[11] *Scripture Hymns*, 1:279, Hymn 881:1 and 2:11, Hymn 1178; *Works*, 7, Hymn 398:1 and 4. Emphasis added.

[12] C. Wesley, *Hymns for Children* (Bristol, 1763), pp. 35–6, Hymn 40:2–3; *Works*, 7, Hymn 461:2–3. Emphasis added.

[13] *HSP* (1742), pp. 44–5, stanzas 4–5, 7–8; *Works*, 7, Hymn 105:3–4, 6–7.

[14] *Scripture Hymns*, 2:170, Hymn 171, lines 5–8; *Works*, 7, Hymn 396:8.

[15] *Scripture Hymns*, 2:89, Hymn 1376; *Works*, 7, Hymn 333:2.

[16] For works that provide analysis of Charles Wesley's doctrine of sanctification and perfect love, see J. Rattenbury, *The Evangelical Doctrines of Charles Wesley's Hymns* (London, 1941), pp. 278–307, and Chilcote, *A Faith That Sings*, pp. 60–70, 122–37. The most important comprehensive examination of this theme is J. Tyson, *Charles Wesley on Sanctification: A Biographical and Theological Study* (Grand Rapids MI, 1986). Several articles also explore this doctrine in the theology of Charles Wesley: J. Tyson, '"The One Thing Needful": Charles Wesley on Sanctification' in *Wesleyan Theological Journal*, vol. 45, no. 2 (2010), 177–95; P. W. Chilcote, '"All the Image of Thy Love": Charles Wesley's Vision of the One Thing Needful', *Proceedings of the Charles Wesley Society*, vol. 18 (2014), 21–40; S T Kimbrough, Jr., 'Charles Wesley and the Journey of Sanctification', *Evangelical Journal*, vol. 16 (1998), 49–75; R. Nicholson, 'The Holiness Emphasis in the Wesleys' Hymns', *Wesleyan Theological Journal*, vol. 5, no. 1 (1970), 49–61; and J. Watson, 'The Presentation of Holiness and the

Concept of Christian Perfection in the Sermons and Hymns of the Wesleys, 1730–1780', in *Transforming Holiness* (Dudley MA, 2006), pp. 81–94.

[17] *HSP* (1742), pp. 30–1, on Psalm 51, stanzas 1, 4 and 8; *Works*, 7, Hymn 334:1, 4 and 8.

[18] C. Wesley, *Hymns and Sacred Poems*, 2 vols. (Bristol, 1749), 2:246, Hymn 418:2, hereinafter *HSP* (1749); cf. *Works*, 7, Hymn 465:2.

[19] *Scripture Hymns*, 1:4, Hymn 5, on Genesis 1:26; *Works*, 7, Hymn 357:4.

[20] *HSP* (1742), 223; *Works*, 7, Hymn 345:13.

[21] For Wesley, a restored loving spirit is 'the one thing needful', and his famous sermon of this title provides a helpful outline for an exploration of holiness and sanctification from his perspective. See K. G. C. Newport, *The Sermons of Charles Wesley: A Critical Edition with Introduction and Notes* (Oxford, 2001), pp. 360–8.

[22] In this section I develop themes first explored in an article entitled '"Claim Me for Thy Service": Charles Wesley's Vision of Servant Vocation', *Proceedings of the Charles Wesley Society*, vol. 11 (2006–7), 69–85.

[23] *HSP* (1749), 2:179; *Works*, 7, Hymn 25:7.

[24] *HSP* (1742), 240–1, stanza 4; *Works*, 7, Hymn 390:2.

[25] *Trinity Hymns*, 99, Hymn 14:4; *Works*, 7, Hymn 253:4.

[26] *Trinity Hymns*, 58, Hymn 87:3; *Works*, 7, Hymn 248:6.

[27] *HSP* (1749), 2:279; Hymn 203:3; *Works*, 7, Hymn 496:3.

[28] Perry Shaw, 'Holistic and Transformative: Beyond a Typological Approach to Theological Education', *Evangelical Review of Theology*, vol. 40, no. 3 (2016), 211.

[29] *HSP* (1749), 2:279; Hymn 203:3; *Works*, 7, Hymn 496:3.

[30] *Scripture Hymns*, 1:316, Hymn 989:2; *Works*, 7, Hymn 436:2.

[31] See S T Kimbrough, Jr., 'Charles Wesley and the Poor', in M. Meeks (ed.), *The Portion of the Poor: Good News to the Poor in the Wesleyan Tradition* (Nashville TN, 1995), pp. 147–67.

[32] *Scripture Hymns*, 2:380, Hymn 738:2; *Works*, 7, Hymn 354:4.

[33] C. Wesley, *Hymns and Sacred Poems* (London, 1739), p. 187, stanza 12; *Works*, 7, Hymn 445:1. See the note on this hymn in *Works*, 7:623–4.

[34] C. Wesley, *Hymns for the Nativity of our Lord* (London, 1745), p. 23, Hymn 18:1; *Works*, 7, Hymn 211:1.

[35] See the Editorial Introduction to this collection of hymns: https://divinity.duke.edu/sites/divinity.duke.edu/files/documents/cswt/54_Hymns_for_the_Year_1756_Mod.pdf (accessed 24 November 2023).

[36] C. Wesley, *Hymns for the Year 1756; Particularly for the Fast-Day, February 6* (Bristol, 1756), p. 22, Hymn 15:5; hereinafter *Hymns for the Year 1756*; cf. *Works*, 7, Hymn 59:3.

[37] *Hymns for the Year 1756*, p. 23, Hymn 16:3–4; *Works*, 7, Hymn 60:3–4.

[38] C. Wesley, *Hymns for those that seek, and those that have Redemption in the Blood of Jesus Christ* (London, 1747), p. 61, Hymn 48:6–8, hereinafter *Redemption Hymns*; cf. *Works*, 7, Hymn 522:6–8.

[39] *Scripture Hymns*, 2:432; Hymn 870:5; *Works*, 7, Hymn 512:5. Emphasis added.

[40] *Scripture Hymns*, 1:58, 188; *Works*, 7, Hymn 309:1.

[41] In addition to the resources listed in n. 1 above, see several of my previous articles that examine the Wesleyan paradigm of renewal from multiple angles: P. W. Chilcote, 'The Wesleyan Revival and Methodism in Cuba', *Quarterly Review*, vol. 17, no. 3 (1997), 207–21; Chilcote, 'An Early Methodist Community of Women', *Methodist History*, vol. 38, no. 4 (2000), 219–30; Chilcote, 'Wesleyan and Emergent Christians in Conversation: A Modest Proposal', *The Epworth Review*, vol. 36, no. 3 (2009), 6–25; and Chilcote, 'Lessons from the

Songs of renewal

"Society Planting" Paradigm of Early Methodist Women', *Witness: Journal of the Academy for Evangelism in Theological Education*, vol 27 (2013), 5–30.

[42] This classic tract is available in many editions and multiple formats. A digital version may be found at https://wesleyscholar.com/wp-content/uploads/2018/09/Character-of-Methodist-1st-ed-1742.pdf (accessed 24 November 2023). See also Steve Harper's concise and compelling summary of the characteristics Wesley sets forth in the document: *Five Marks of a Methodist: The Fruit of a Living Faith* (Nashville TN, 2015).

[43] C. Wesley, 'Primitive Christianity', in John Wesley, *An Earnest Appeal to Men of Reason and Religion*, second edition (Bristol, 1743), pp. 52–5; cf. *Works*, 7, Hymns 16 and 17.

[44] C. Wesley, *Hymns for the Use of Families* (Bristol, 1767), p. 14, Hymn 12:2; *Works*, 7, Hymn 477:2.

[45] *HSP* (1749), 1:248, Hymn 147:4–5; *Works*, 7, Hymn 495:4–5.

[46] The editors of the definitive edition of the *Collection* indicate the potential connection here with Antoinette Bourginon and the similar question she poses in *Light of the World*. See *Works*, 7:99, notes on the respective lines.

[47] See P. W. Chilcote, 'The Wesleyan Tradition: A Paradigm of Renewal for the Contemporary Church', in Chilcote (ed.), *The Wesleyan Tradition*, pp. 23–37.

[48] *Scripture Hymns*, 2:25; Hymn 1211:1; *Works*, 7, Hymn 172:2.

[49] *Scripture Hymns*, 1:331; Hymn 1025:1; *Works*, 7, Hymn 454:1.

[50] *Scripture Hymns*, 2:13–14; Hymn 1185:1–2; *Works*, 7, Hymn 91:1–2. The second stanza quoted here does not appear in the *Collection* but is included from the original for emphasis. In the *Collection*, the original eight-line stanzas were subdivided into two four-line stanzas.

[51] *Scripture Hymns*, 1:391; Hymn 1157:1; *Works*, 7, Hymn 440:1.

[52] *Scripture Hymns*, 1:391–2; Hymns 1157, 1158, and 1159; *Works*, 7, Hymn 440:2–5.

[53] *Redemption Hymns*, p. 52; Hymn 41:8; *Works*, 7, Hymn 69:6.

[54] See my discussion of this central rediscovery of the Wesleys in P. W. Chilcote, 'The Mission-Church Paradigm of the Wesleyan Revival', in D. Whiteman and G. Anderson (eds), *World Mission in the Wesleyan Spirit* (Franklin, TN, 2009), pp. 151–64 and Chilcote, 'Missio Dei and the Wesleyan Mission-Church Paradigm', in Kathy Armistead (ed.), Missio Dei *in the United States: Toward a Faithful United Methodist Witness* (Nashville TN, 2018), pp. 23–38.

[55] Chilcote, *A Faith That Sings*, p. 116.

[56] C. Wesley, *Hymns on the Lord's Supper* (Bristol, 1745), p. 129, Hymn 155:3; *Works*, 7, Hymn 418:3.

[57] *HSP* (1749), 1:311, Hymn 197:11; *Works*, 7, Hymn 38:6. Emphasis added.

CHARLES WESLEY AND ARCHAIC SYMBOLISM[1]

Pauline Watson

This essay takes a new and different look at why Charles Wesley's hymns are felt to be so helpful to us in our human predicament. Why do they so effectively stimulate our religious imagination, expand our spiritual awareness, and enable our spiritual and emotional growth? Most previous study of why this is the case has been concerned with Wesley's facility with language, his use of words and figures of speech, which was often idiosyncratic; and with his ability to convey complicated theological concepts in poetry. The words could then be set to music and sung in a doxological setting of praise and prayer. Because of this poetic and doxological setting, those who sing his hymns often respond powerfully, not only on a cognitive level but in some way which is beyond the cognitive. This essay suggests that, in addition to the music and the worship setting, this relates to some extent to Wesley's treatment of Christian symbolism; and in order to extend our understanding of how this might happen, it uses psychoanalytic theory to examine the processes involved.

Keywords: Charles Wesley, hymns, theology, Julia Kristeva, Paul Ricoeur

The theologian Paul Tillich argued that Christian symbolism could open us to something beyond ourselves, but also to something within us.[2] Similarly, the philosopher Paul Ricoeur suggested that the force and richness of religious symbolism is attributable to the inseparability of two ways of interpreting its action: the interpretation of symbols in a way which points to what is beyond us (what he called 'progressive' interpretation – the way theologians usually interpret symbols), and a reading of symbols which evokes very early (or 'archaic') human experience, what he called 'archaeological', or 'regressive' interpretation.[3]

https://doi.org/10.16922/jrhlc.10.2.4

In the first part of this essay, I elucidate ways in which Charles Wesley's treatment of symbolism might point to something beyond us (Ricoeur's progressive hermeneutic). This involves the study of the work of literary scholars, who have explored his use of words in detail, and the recognition of a variety of linguistic devices in his poetry. It also draws a comparison with the ways in which the Early Fathers understood their search for God, which I suggest have some parallels with the ways in which Wesley's hymns can open our spiritual experience to what is beyond us, to the transcendent. In the second part, I will explore the ways in which Wesley's treatment of Christian symbolism can evoke early human experience (Ricoeur's regressive hermeneutic). In this second part I shall use psychoanalytic thinking, particularly the work of the French professor of linguistics and psychoanalyst Julia Kristeva. This I hope will enlarge our understanding of how the hymns affect us, not only consciously, but unconsciously. Through an exploration of these two ways in which it is possible to interpret the symbolism of the hymns, it should become clearer how their 'double' action (the inseparability of their two actions) adds to their power.

'Progressive' interpretation

In their search for the divine, the Early Fathers described a process which involved pushing the intellect as far as it would go (I refer particularly to Dionysius the Areopagite, the late fifth-century Greek speaking Syrian, as an example). He described how, initially in this search, an attempt should be made to find the words in which to describe God. This is an impossible task, and so these attempts must inevitably fail. They must therefore be denied; however, the description in words resulting from the denial can also only fail, and so this too must be denied. In the example Denys Turner gives in *The Darkness of God*, the first affirmation is 'God is Light'. This is inadequate to describe God and must be denied, so it becomes 'God is Darkness'. Again, this is inadequate so must be negated, becoming 'God is brilliant darkness'.[4] This is a paradoxical and unresolvable statement. As Turner comments, it is not just an artful form of language but *deliberately* paradoxical. Affirmation and denial are collapsed into what he describes as 'self-subverting' speech, which leads to a perplexing silence beyond words. This strenuous intellectual struggle with words is known as a 'cataphatic' process. It gives way to an 'apophatic' realm which is beyond words. As Turner describes the process, 'It is on the other side of both our affirmations and our denials that the silence of the transcendent is glimpsed, seen through the fissures opened up in our language by the dialectical strategy of self-subversion'.[5] This is a realm of unknowing, of silence beyond language, of bewilderment, where preconceptions have to be given up, a moment of 'negativity', a moment of aliveness and risk; there is no knowing where it will lead. The apophatic realm is not a realm of intense emotional experience but one of loss, tension and anxiety. For the Early Fathers, the two processes, the cataphatic and the apophatic, were interwoven throughout their religious practice.[6]

Although not based on the collapsing of 'affirmation' and denial, Donald Davie's explorations of Charles Wesley's use of language evoke these descriptions of pushing the intellect to the limit by the use of 'self-subverting' speech. While he acknowledges that Wesley is a poet of 'vehement feeling', he also suggests that the intellectual effort required is important in the powerful effect of his hymns. For Davie, paradoxically, Wesley's 'strong and muscular thought' does not dry up emotion but intensifies it, and the pushing of thought and reason as far as they can go, in an attempt to understand what is beyond words, leads to a place of silence, of unknowing and perplexity. As with the cataphatic struggles of the early mystics, when reason and logic reach their limit, the singer of Wesley's hymns arrives at such a place. This is achieved through Wesley's use of such devices as paradox, metaphor, words with ambiguous meaning, neologisms, and the condensing of complex concepts or images into very few words. There is also a sudden use of what Davie calls 'poignant simplicity'.[7] An example that he cites is:

> Jesus is come, your common Lord;
> Pardon ye all through Him may have,
> May now be saved, whoever will;
> This Man receiveth sinners still.[8]

The sudden direct appearance of 'this Man' as a way of describing Jesus Christ, and the simple word 'still', surprises and shocks, and pulls us up short.

The great paradox of Christian faith is of course the Incarnation: in Wesley's words: 'Being's Source *begins to* Be, / And GOD himself is Born!'[9] When comparing Wesley's use of paradox, with that of the fourth-century priest and hymn writer, Ephrem the Syrian, Kimbrough writes that we can 'live the paradox of the Incarnation, live the mystery', but we cannot resolve it; we can 'live' it, by being indwelt by God's kenotic love as shown in the Incarnation, and by showing it in relationships with others. Although we cannot resolve it intellectually, and it remains a mystery, it can change how we live.[10] And Wesley's hymns are saturated with such paradoxes: God is hidden but shown, veiled but unveiled, the immortal dies, the invisible appears, immortal bread, victim divine, unbloody sacrifice, 'Impassive He suffers, Immortal He dies', are just a few examples. All of which make us pause, perplexed, having to think again, and see the richness of their contradictions afresh.

Wesley also uses words with ambiguous meanings, which can extend our thought: Francis Frost discusses one such example. He suggests that Wesley deliberately makes use of the Greek word for 'taste', γεύομαι, in the New Testament, which can be understood either in the material sense, of tasting food, or in a spiritual sense:

> Might we not all by Faith obtain
> By Faith the Mountain-sin remove,
> Enjoy the sense of sins forgiven,
> And Holiness, the Taste of Heaven?[11]

Frost convincingly argues that the use of 'taste' in this context is mainly to portray the beauty and intensity of the Moravian experience of the divine, but that also there are overtones of the Eucharist. There are echoes too of the psalms: 'O taste and see that the Lord is good' (Psalm 34:8); and of the Heavenly manna given to the Israelites in the desert. In addition, it evokes the experience of the child at the breast, as described in the first book of Peter: 'As newborn babes, desire the sincere milk of the word, that ye may grow thereby: If so be ye have tasted that the Lord is gracious.' (King James Version, 1 Peter 2:2–3).[12] In this one word 'taste' the spiritual and the physical (even the primitive, the breast-feeding baby), are brought together. Similarly, the word 'antepast' ('foretaste') is used in 'Where shall my wond'ring Soul begin?', in which Wesley describes his 'knowing' and 'feeling' that his sins are forgiven as 'an Antepast of Heaven'. Here feeling, knowing and tasting, the intellectual, spiritual and physical are all involved.[13]

Wesley's hymns are full of metaphors, many of them biblical: 'Love's redeeming work is done, / Fought the fight the battle won', Jesus as the good Shepherd or the spotless lamb, Christ the medicine of the broken heart. Davie suggests that he did not coin many 'novel' metaphors but was adept at refreshing dead ones. For instance: 'Strike with the Hammer of thy Word, / And break these Hearts of Stone'.[14] He also describes how, through his very precise use of words and their placing in relation to other words – as a contrast, as an antithesis, or in juxtaposition—we are forced to think harder than usual about their meanings.[15] Wesley also arrests attention by using neologisms, such as: 'implunged in the crystal abyss' if he thought it necessary.[16] 'Implunged', a rare word, is used on twelve occasions in his hymns.

In addition, complex theological concepts are often condensed into very few words. There is a striking example on the Trinity, quoted by Campbell:

> Hail Father, Son and Spirit, great
> before the birth of time,
> Inthron'd in everlasting state
> Jehovah Elohim!
>
> A mystical plurality
> We in the Godhead own,
> Adoring One in Persons Three
> And Three in Nature One.[17]

As Campbell points out, he uses all the technical terms 'Nature', 'Persons' and 'Elohim' (the Hebrew name for God in plural form) indicating the plurality of the Divine Persons, and includes their 'co-eternality', all within thirty-five words.[18]

All these devices lead to an opening up of the mind to a place of aliveness, questioning and uncertainty. Like the effect of the 'self-subverting speech' of Dionysius the Areopagite, Charles Wesley's use of words in his poems, and his use of paradox and other devices in his treatment of Christian symbolism and narrative, involve a stretching of the intellect to a place of unknowing. They draw us on to something beyond ourselves. 'Unsearchable' and 'unspeakable' were two of Wesley's favourite words:

> Unsearchable the Love
> That hath the Saviour brought,
> The Grace is far above

Or Men or Angels Thought;
Suffice for Us, that GOD, we know,
Our GOD is manifest below.[19]

Though here the unsearchable becomes 'manifest' in the incarnation, God made flesh in a baby.

The devices Wesley uses with words and syntax in his hymns are of course not specific to Charles Wesley's poetry but are features of poetic language more generally. This style of writing is sometimes described as 'doing violence to language' or as a 'special' poetic language which is different from the mundane speech of everyday life.[20] It is a form of writing which recalls what Kristeva calls *écriture*. As Kearns explains, Kristeva 'counterposes' *écriture* to theology, which she sees as logocentric and as capable of 'blinding' rather than enlightening when 'it is taken for a transparent representation of the absolute truth'. *Écriture* on the other hand does not avoid its own 'concrete, fallen, fractured and mortal nature.'[21] It allows an expression of the body as well as the soul; the subject is mortal and speaking. It allows what Kristeva, using words in her own idiosyncratic way, calls the 'semiotic', the realm of the body and of wordless infancy, to break into the 'symbolic' realm of words, rules and logic of the theological text.

This special language, evident in Wesley's hymns, in addition to bringing us to Dionysius's 'apophatic' place, can also be seen as connected to early experience and feeling, through its allowing 'semiotic' elements to break through. And this return to a realm before speech leads to the second part of this essay, which considers Ricoeur's other mode of interpretation of symbols, the regressive interpretation.

Archaeological interpretation

Kristeva is interested in the way in which Christian symbol and narrative can evoke our inner experience. Although not a believer, she has a great deal of insight and understanding into the way in which Christian symbols resonate with the early human experiences and with the struggles we all have to negotiate. The feelings, wishes and impulses she describes are those of infancy, but how well we manage to negotiate our way through them has a profound effect on us throughout our lives.

As most of us will have witnessed, a young baby's feelings are passionate: the seizing of the breast as if to devour it, the rage at being left hungry, at not being picked up, or held, or changed, or in response to a colicky pain; and the peace and contentment after a good feed. The child's first carer, usually the mother, in the period before the child has words, helps him/her to deal with these mainly bodily aspects and their associated primitive feelings. If she is well 'attuned' to the baby, she uses close attention, sensitive responses, and her own words, to help him/her make sense of his/her feelings. Many factors, both in the baby and the mother, can interfere with this process.

At a slightly later stage, the child must deal with the loves, hates and jealousies of the period when she or he realizes that her/his parents are a couple and that she/he is excluded from their adult relationship. The adjustment to, and acceptance of, this state of affairs is not easy, but is less problematic if the earlier mother/child interaction has gone well. All of us vary in how well we deal with this stormy Oedipal period, and in how well our parents are able to help us through it. We also vary in how well we cope with unresolved feelings from infancy when they are stirred up in future relationships throughout life. Sometimes they are so difficult, shaming and unresolved at the early stage that they have to be firmly kept out of consciousness. When this is the case they might nevertheless give rise to psychological symptoms, or unhelpful repetitive patterns of behaviour.

Kristeva has written extensively about the many resonances and parallels between Christian symbolism and early experience. Her writing is in French; she writes lyrically, poetically, and sometimes personally. She plays with words, often using them idiosyncratically. This oblique and often ambiguous writing makes her difficult to translate and to read, and it is particularly difficult to attempt to paraphrase her thoughts without sounding facile or banal. I am aware that if her ideas are baldly stated, particularly to people not accustomed to psychoanalytic thinking, they can appear far-fetched or even ridiculous. However, I am reluctant to allow these difficulties to deprive us of what I think are important pointers to how an interaction with the Christian narrative, Christian symbolism and sacrament can affect a believer at a deep level and will risk two or three examples.

Kristeva draws attention to the emphasis on bread, and on physical and spiritual hunger in chapters 6 and 8 of St Mark's Gospel. This is the story of feeding the five thousand, and of Jesus's subsequent discussion of it with his disciples. She links it to Christ's later saying, 'This is my body broken for you' and to the eating of bread, the body of Christ in the Eucharist. These references evoke themes of 'devouring' and 'satiation'. I have already mentioned the very young baby's screaming for food and 'devouring' the breast, and its peace and contentment after a good feed. Kristeva describes these two primitive impulses (devouring and satiation) as 'surreptitiously mingled' as the sacrament is offered.[22] Or in Charles Wesley's hymn:

> He bids us drink and eat
> Imperishable Food;
> He gives his Flesh to be our Meat,
> And bids us drink his Blood.
> Whate'er th'Almighty can
> To pardon'd sinners give,
> The Fulness of our God made man
> We here with CHRIST receive.[23]

Charles Wesley does not flinch from our eating flesh and drinking blood, but in the last verse we are full, forgiven, and Christ is alive with us. For Kristeva, this acting out, this performing of what is forbidden, the eating the bread, the body, the devouring, takes the destructive guilt out of the forbidden impulse. It is different, but nevertheless similar, I think, to the catharsis of a Greek tragedy. Following Aristotle, Karen Armstrong describes this as: 'an interior purification resulting from the violent invasion of the heart and mind by the emotions of pity and terror'. There is an identification with the pain and suffering of another so that the 'scope of their sympathy and humanity' are enlarged.[24]

Psychoanalysts describe a 'melancholy period' in the infant's life after birth, during a process of separating and feeling torn away from the mother, and before the acquisition of language. It is a period of loneliness and insecurity, of powerful feelings, as we have seen, and fear of death, remnants of which remain in the unconscious as the child grows. The child has to be helped to separate from the mother, the early world of the body and bodily fluids, of touching, feeding, and cleaning, and to move towards a realm of thinking and speaking. There is a fear of being sucked back in to the world before words, and hence to the realm of chaos and meaninglessness. If all goes well the infant learns to use words, through which to understand and come to terms with his/her feelings. The child eventually finds language, meaning and the beginnings of a sense of self, an identity, within the loving relationship with his/her parents. Kristeva cites the suffering, crucified Christ as a figure who can symbolise this 'melancholy' infant for the believer. Christ's kenotic separation from God, his suffering and subsequent death, parallel the infant's journey in the search for meaning and identity. Christ is rewarded with life, is absorbed into the Trinity and receives a 'Name' (language and his true identity). He is absorbed into a realm of truth and meaning; into a realm in which we no longer see through a glass darkly, but face to face. Similarly, the suffering believer struggling to find acceptance, meaning and truth, who identifies with Christ, is rewarded through God's agapeic love as shown in Christ:

> Thy causeless unexhausted love,
> Unmerited and free,
> Delights our evil to remove,
> And help our misery.[25]

We sing this usually as it refers to our present lives, in which we are often struggling but as these parallels show, it can resonate at a deeper, unconscious level.

The theologian Graham Ward has looked at these resonances between God's kenosis and Kristeva's understanding of the child's experience after separation from the mother and up to the acquisition of language. He describes both narratives as 'allegories of love'. Because of their deep resonances, in Ward's words, the believer is 'caught up not in a knowledge but a knowing of God, a revelation about God that issues from the movement of his intra-Trinitarian love.'[26] It is a kind of knowledge which is beyond words and logic, and which engages the believer at a deep level. This is similar to Ricoeur's description of the strength of symbols being ascribable to their regressive as well as progressive effects.

Charles Wesley, of course, wrote many hymns based on the Trinity. As we have seen, he included all the technicalities of Trinitarian theology, often in very condensed form; but as in 'Love Divine, all Loves excelling', which also had a Trinitarian structure (until the verse 'Breathe, O breathe thy loving spirit', was cut by John), the emphasis was on love; the love of the Trinity, mirrored in the 'archaic' triangle.[27] It is these very early resonances which I think allow Christian symbolism to move us at a very deep level, often an unconscious level, and to facilitate change.

I have talked a lot about powerful feelings which belong to infancy; but I have also stressed their effect on us throughout life. If these feelings have been well negotiated and resolved in infancy and childhood, we are then free to respond to each new experience in a flexible and creative way. For some people however, their early experience has been so unsatisfactory that they have not learned how to make sense of their feelings or put them into words. As a result, when the primitive chaotic feelings, urges and wishes originating in early experience are stirred up by events or in later relationships, they can be so disturbing, provoking anxiety, guilt or shame, that they have to be firmly kept out of consciousness. This sometimes leads to an inappropriate acting out of the feelings, or they are pushed out and attributed to somebody else. They cannot be faced up to and tolerated. Such difficulty in putting feelings into thoughts or words, that is, in using words as symbols, can extend to an inability to relate to symbols more generally. Those who have not learned how to symbolise might therefore not be touched by the resonances of symbols, or might feel so disturbed by them, that they would prefer to avoid them. At the other extreme, some creative people, some artists and poets, seem particularly good at accessing unconscious material and giving it form in their work. Most of us lie somewhere in between.

My research into the early experience of John and Charles has looked at where they might lie on this spectrum. It is not possible to address the many factors influencing my findings here, but I concluded that for Charles the very early years of his life were easier than they were for John. For reasons related to Susanna's state of mind, including the effects of the deaths of many of her children, the two brothers' positions in the family in relation to these deaths, and her own early experience and marriage, I concluded that there would have been fewer unrealistic expectations on Charles, and that Susanna would have been more available to him emotionally than she was for John. If Susanna was more closely attuned to Charles, then the early stages of resolving his chaotic primitive feelings would have progressed more smoothly, so that these feelings would have felt less threatening and disturbing for him than for John. He would have had less need to keep them out of consciousness and so more able to use symbols in his hymns which resonated with early feelings. He was not afraid to use bodily, 'carnal' images which evoke very early, pre-language experience from the maternal realm, of the child torn from the maternal body, of blood, water and wounds, and of feeding, tasting, devouring:

Father, see the Victim slain,
Jesus Christ, the Just, the Good,
Offer'd up for guilty Man,
Pouring out his precious Blood;
Him, and then the Sinner see,
Look through Jesu's Wounds on Me.[28]

Nor did he flinch from images of love, merging and boundlessness, which again evoke primitive longings. John on the other hand was more ambivalent: while he translated German hymns which included the language of love, of boundless heights and abysses and suggested a primitive wish to merge in a blissful, ecstatic state, and while he gladly sang Charles's hymns, he struggled with the Moravians' stress on blood and wounds and anything too visceral. He found what he called 'namby-pambical' baby talk and 'fondling expressions' very difficult, and tended to edit them out of Charles hymns.[29] This suggests that they evoked early unresolved painful experience and feelings, which he preferred to keep walled off.

Although Kristeva has written a great deal about how Christian symbolism resonates with unconscious material, she suggests that unlike some early mystics, particularly Bernard of Clairvaux, of whom she approves, most *contemporary* forms of religion forget their affective and bodily aspects and so do not fully deal with the primitive urges, impurities and evils of humanity, what she calls the 'abject'. As she describes it, in the contemporary forms the 'abject' is verbalised as 'sin' and after repentance and sanctification through the taking in of the body of Christ in Communion, sin is forgiven and wiped away by absolution; this becomes the starting point for the journey to redemption. But she reminds us that the Christian remains a divided and so 'lapsing' subject and therefore must repeatedly confess and take communion. In Kristeva's view this means that the true horror and chaos of the 'abject' is glossed over rather than fully faced and examined, or in her words 'elaborated'.[30]

While Kristeva's charge of 'glossing over the 'abject' may be true in some forms of contemporary worship, the exploration of the use of archaic symbols in Charles Wesley's hymns suggests that his hymns in particular do not gloss over our carnal and affective aspects (those aspects which come from within), but they do 'elaborate' them. Early experiences are evoked by his use of sounds and rhythms (those perceptions that infants first respond to), by oral images of tasting, feeding, satiety and devouring. And there are abundant corporeal metaphors of killing, woundedness, brokenness, messiness and touching. For instance, there is a verse full if murderousness:

> O what a killing Thought is This,
> A Sword to pierce the faithful Heart!
> Our Sins have slain the Prince of Peace;
> Our Sins which caused this mortal Smart,
> With Him we vow to crucify;
> Our Sins which murdered GOD shall die![31]

Or a hymn in which images of pollution and woundedness are interlaced with those of saving love:

> I am all unclean, unclean
> Thy Purity I want;
> My whole Heart is sick of Sin,
> And my whole Head is faint:
> Full of putrifying Sores,
> Of Bruises, and of Wounds my Soul
> Looks to JESUS; Help implores,
> And gasps to be made whole.[32]

The 'badness' here cannot be seen as avoided or glossed over; rather Wesley appears to have elaborated it vividly.

Conclusion

We have seen from Kristeva's thinking that the Christian narratives, symbols and sacraments can symbolise hidden, often feared and unresolved feelings and experience. They are therefore likely to move us at a deeper level than we might expect, and possibly also promote some resolution through bringing these elements nearer to consciousness and offering a new opportunity to consider them. This is an opening up to what is within us, and it is a use of symbols that is particularly apparent in the hymns of Charles Wesley. From the first part of the essay, we learned how his hymns could also be seen as opening us up to something beyond ourselves.

The hymns could be said to fulfil both of Tillich's predictions: firstly, they move us by opening us up to something beyond ourselves, to an intuiting of the transcendent. This is like the interaction of the cataphatic and the apophatic of the early mystics (Ricoeur's progressive interpretation). And secondly, they also open us up to the depths of our personality, to what is within us, by evoking early feeling and experience, both through his style of writing, his *écriture*, and his treatment of Christian symbolism (Ricoeur's regressive interpretation).

Kristeva writes that Christian symbolism 'supplies images for even the fissures in our secret and fundamental logic' and so she concludes that it is not surprising that people believe the Christian narrative.[33] Given Charles Wesley's ability to access his own unconscious, and to use words and images in ways which move us at a deep level, we might say that it is also not surprising that we enjoy and often have a sense of being challenged, or healed and affirmed, when we sing his hymns.

Notes

[1] Many of the ideas outlined in this essay are discussed more fully in the author's book about growth and change in a religious context exemplified in the lives of John and Charles Wesley: P. E. Watson, *'Two Scrubby Travellers': A Psychoanalytic View of Flourishing and Constraint in Religion through the Lives of John and Charles Wesley* (London and New York, 2018).

[2] P. Tillich, *Systematic Theology II* (London, 1957), p. 190.

[3] P. Ricoeur, *Freud and Philosophy: An Essay in Interpretation* (New Haven and London, 1970), p. 496.

[4] D. Turner, *The Darkness of God: Negativity in Christian Mysticism* (Cambridge, 1995), p. 22.

[5] Ibid, p. 45.

[6] Ibid, p. 265.

[7] D. Davie, *Purity of Diction in English Verse* (Cambridge, 1967), pp. 72–3.

[8] *Hymns on God's Everlasting Love* (1756), Hymn 10, 'Jesus Christ the Saviour of all Men'.

[9] *Hymns for the Nativity of our Lord* (1745), Hymn 4, 'Glory be to God on high'.

[10] S T Kimbrough, Jr., 'Kenosis in the Nativity Hymns of Ephrem the Syrian and Charles Wesley', in S T Kimbrough, Jr. (ed.), *Orthodox and Wesleyan Spirituality* (Crestwood NY, 2002), pp. 280–3.

[11] *Hymns on the Lord's Supper* (1745), Hymn 54, 'Why did my Dying Lord ordain'.

[12] F. Frost, 'The Eucharistic Hymns of Charles Wesley: "The Self-Emptying Glory of God"' in *Proceedings of the Charles Wesley Society*, vol. 2 (1995), 91–2.

[13] *Hymns and Sacred Poems* (1739), Part II, Hymn 1, 'CHRIST the Friend of Sinners'.

[14] *Hymns and Sacred Poems* (1749), vol. 1, Hymn 201, 'Written before Preaching at Portland'.

[15] Davie, *Purity of Diction*, pp. 72–3.

[16] *Short Hymns on Select Passages of the Holy Scriptures*, vol. II, Hymn 865, 'The thirsty are called to their Lord', on Revelation 22:17.

[17] *Hymns on the Trinity* (1767), Hymn 87, 'Hail Father, Son and Spirit, great'.

[18] T. A. Campbell, 'Charles Wesley, *Theologos*' in K. G. C. Newport and T. A. Campbell (eds), *Charles Wesley: Life, literature and legacy* (Peterborough, 2007), pp. 266–7.

[19] *Hymns for the Nativity of our Lord* (1745). Hymn 5, 'Let Earth and Heaven combine'.

[20] J. R. Watson, '"Sorrow and Love, Love and Sorrow": The Poetics of Hymnody since the Reformation', *The Hymn* (Hymn Society in the United States and Canada), vol. 68, no. 4 (Autumn 2017), 37.

[21] C. McNelly Kearns, 'Art and Religious Discourse in Aquinas and Kristeva' in D. Crownfield (ed.), *Body Text in Julia Kristeva: Religion, women and psychoanalysis* (Albany NY, 1992), pp. 113–17.

[22] J. Kristeva, *Powers of Horror*, trans. L. Roudiez (New York, 1982), pp. 114–20.

[23] *Hymns on the Lord's Supper* (1745), Hymn 81, 'Jesu, we Thus obey'.

[24] K. Armstrong, *A Short History of Myth* (Edinburgh, New York and London, 2005), p. 100.

[25] *Short Hymns on Select Passages of the Holy Scriptures*, vol. I, Hymn 169, on Exodus 34:6.

[26] G. Ward, 'Kenosis and Naming' in P. Heelas (ed.), *Religion, Modernity and Postmodernity* (Oxford, 1998), pp. 251–3.

[27] *Hymns for those that Seek, and those that have Redemption in the Blood of Jesus Christ* (1747), Hymn 9, 'Love Divine, all Loves excelling'.

[28] *Hymns on the Lord's Supper* (1745), Hymn 120, 'Father see the Victim slain'.

[29] F. Baker, *Representative Verse of Charles Wesley* (London, 1962), p. 59.

[30] Kristeva, *Powers of Horror*, pp. 113–19.

[31] *Hymns on the Lord's Supper* (1745), Hymn 133, 'O Thou, who hast our Sorrows took'.

[32] *Hymns and Sacred Poems* (1742), [no hymn number] 'Wretched, helpless and distressed', pp. 43–4.

[33] J. Kristeva, *In the Beginning Was Love: Psychoanalysis and Faith*, trans. A. Goldhammer (New York, 1997), pp. 41–2.

MUSIC AND CHARLES WESLEY'S LEGACY

Martin V. Clarke

Charles Wesley is one of the most prominent figures in the history of Methodism, arguably second only in the popular imagination to his older brother, John. In large part, this is due to Charles's prolific achievements as a hymn writer. A significant number of his hymns, albeit a small proportion of the estimated nine thousand he wrote, have been widely and continuously sung in worship by Methodists and other Christians in Great Britain and beyond since the eighteenth century. Charles's hymn texts were written to be sung, whether by the early followers of Methodism in the small group meetings that were integral to the movement's structure, or in the public worship of the Church of England, which the early Methodist leaders sought to reinvigorate. Most people, within and beyond Methodism, who have encountered Charles Wesley's religious poetry since the mid-eighteenth century have done so through participating in hymn singing or by hearing others do so.

Keywords: Charles Wesley, Methodism, music, hymns, singing, multimedia

Charles Wesley's accomplishments as a hymn writer have contributed to his legacy in several ways. The sheer volume and thematic range of his output and the specificity of some of his hymns with regard to particular places or events indicate the extent to which hymns were embedded within early Methodist life, helped by his memorable use of language. Examples of his work are strongly associated with seasons of the Christian year, or particular events in his life that resonated with later believers, such as religious conversion. Striking words and phrases such as the polysyllabic 'inextinguishable' in 'O thou, who camest from above', and 'lost in wonder, love and praise' in 'Love divine, all loves excelling' demonstrate his poetic skill and creativity. Music is

https://doi.org/10.16922/jrhlc.10.2.5

also part of Charles Wesley's reputation, although more peripherally than poetry. In large part, this relates to his family life, and especially the ways in which he encouraged the musical nurturing of two of his children, Charles junior and Samuel.[1] Their achievements as musicians create the impression of a highly musical family, whose prominence was enhanced by the series of concerts performed by Charles junior and Samuel in the family's London home, which attracted renowned musicians from across the capital. Charles's acquaintanceship with several leading figures in London's musical and theatrical community is also a commonly noted strand of his biography beyond his significance as a religious leader.

Studies of Charles Wesley's hymns abound, covering many literary and theological standpoints. Major historical accounts of English-language hymnody typically devote extensive space to discussion of his work; J. R. Watson draws attention to the breadth and depth of Wesley's allusions to the Bible and other literature as well as highlighting striking examples of his poetical craft. More theologically focused studies give prominence to different parts of Wesley's output in terms of their doctrinal or liturgical significance. J. E. Rattenbury, for example, sought to emphasise the sacramental theology of the Wesley brothers partly to reassert Methodism's liturgical heritage in a period when he and others felt this was neglected.[2] The same author also addressed Charles's evangelicalism, highlighting the theological breadth of his output and its significance for Christians across a range of liturgical and ecclesiastical traditions.[3] More recent studies include both examinations of specific parts of Wesley's output and analyses of particular theological themes across his work.[4] These have played a significant role in advancing understanding of Charles Wesley's life, work and theology, and in so doing have defined his distinctive contribution to Methodism, allowing him to emerge from his brother's shadow. Their focus, however, means that they necessarily and justifiably concentrate on the textual content of his hymns with at most passing reference to their combination with music in the practice of singing.

The emphasis on Wesley's texts is reflected in Ted A. Campbell's study of Methodist historiography, *Encoding Methodism: Telling and retelling narratives of Wesleyan origins*. Drawing on metaphors of coding – both in the sense of DNA and computer programming – Campbell identifies a series of 'narrative modules' that are typically found in histories of Wesleyan communities, whether recounted formally or informally:

We can envision this kit of modules as a collection of stories told by preachers and other oral narrators, or written on paper saved in file folders, or written in word-processor files on computer storage media, or saved in the cloud, or perhaps published in a printed or electronically readable book. In many cases the material had been originally transmitted in the memories of the tellers of narratives, encoded memories that were repeated so many times that their accuracy seemed utterly trustworthy to the tellers.[5]

Among the modules Campbell identifies is one referring to Charles Wesley's hymns, which he labels as 'CWPoetry':

A narrative of Charles Wesley's poetic works and their contributions to the Wesleyan movement. A certain selection of Charles Wesley's poetry was often invoked to describe the identity of Methodism as a pietistic expression of Christian faith, though a different selection of Charles Wesley's poetry could also be utilized as a way of building the more traditionally ecclesial or 'high-church' identity of Methodism as liturgically oriented communities.[6]

Both label and description are valid and insightful, as Campbell's analysis of a range of published Methodist histories from the earliest days through to the twenty-first century demonstrates. However, this particular module, with its precise focus on the literary and theological content of Wesley's poetry, does not express the experiential importance of hymn singing, or the significance of Wesley's words being set to music. Campbell's work provides a model for understanding how different interpretations and elements of broader Methodist history have been foregrounded at different points in the movement's history. There are clear parallels with the changing reception of Charles Wesley's hymns, but this essay contends that the singing of hymns, especially but not exclusively those by Charles Wesley, itself needs to be understood as being encoded within Methodist identity.

The importance of the relationship between words and music in hymn singing is recognised in some historical accounts of early Methodism. For example, in *Methodism: Empire of the Spirit*, David Hempton devotes a chapter to 'The Medium and the Message', which includes discussion of the practice of hymnody in response to the question, 'How then was Wesleyan hymnody consumed by Methodists?' Noting the prevalence

59

of hymn singing in eighteenth-century Methodist life, he concludes that 'the medium and the message were in perfect harmony'.[7] Hymnal prefaces attest to this too, setting themselves not only as custodians of Charles Wesley's poetry for each new generation, but also perpetuating Methodism's practice of vital hymn singing. The most potent expression of this is to be found in the opening words of the preface to the 1933 *Methodist Hymn Book*: 'Methodism was born in song'.[8]

In characterising the relationship between medium and message, Hempton is asserting a particular kind of relationship between words and music, which he claims was especially successful and appropriate in eighteenth-century Methodism. Despite this, he comments only briefly on early Methodist musical repertoire, noting 'the appropriation of popular tunes', although these are just one of several tune types found in eighteenth-century Methodist publications.[9] Beyond claiming that hymns gave Methodism a popular appeal based on both content and style, Hempton offers no assessment of what made the music such an apparently fine match for the words. Given both the diverse musical repertoire set to Charles Wesley's hymns in the eighteenth century and the many subsequent changes in the tunes and musical styles associated with them, the relationship between words and music, and in particular the ways in which music contributes to meanings attached to the hymns, demands closer investigation.

Jeremy Begbie provides helpful models for interpreting the relationship between words and music in *Music, Modernity and God: Essays in listening*, especially in two chapters on 'Music and God-Talk', which draw on Nicholas Cook's work on musical multimedia. Building on Cook's argument that music is always encountered as part of a multimedia experience, Begbie pays particular attention to the ways in which words and music interact in relation to theological meaning. As well as using this as a model for understanding the influence of musical settings on the theological meanings associated with Charles Wesley's hymn texts, this article also contends that consideration of the impact of music on perceptions of the meaning of hymn texts is also revealing in terms of cultural and social values and contexts. Begbie begins by setting out how the relationship between music and words is often perceived in Christian contexts through the notion of conformance: 'A combination of music and text will be regarded as successful just to the extent that the media align, accord with each other.'[10] This seems to be what Hempton identifies in his assertions about early Methodist hymn singing. Indeed,

Begbie notes that a particular kind of conformance, labelled 'unitary conformance' by Cook, which accords primacy to one of the elements in a multimedia relationship, has often been regarded as normative and desirable by those writing about Christian worship: in such analyses, 'Music will at best magnify meaning already believed to be present "in" the text'.[11] John Wesley seems to have viewed the relationship of words and music in this way. His essay 'Thoughts on the Power of Music' promotes such a relationship in its criticism of polyphony and its advocacy of textual clarity.[12] Where John Wesley found the relationship not to be such, he tended to be critical, as found both in general terms in his essay and in particular instances recorded in his journal, notably when describing how he corrected the singing practice of one Methodist society he visited, having found it dominated by a small group.[13]

Begbie summarises Cook in outlining the inadequacies of this model, noting how conformance of this kind is almost never complete or sustained: 'Marked discrepancies between music and texts are nearly always present, even when conformance theory is being most strongly advocated.'[14] This is especially obvious in the case of a text consisting of multiple stanzas; mood and imagery may vary considerably across stanzas, rendering a tune deemed to be in conformance with the opening stanza, for instance, to seem incongruous in relation to later stanzas. Moreover, the interchangeability of hymn tunes and texts suggests a more complicated relationship. Wesley wrote metrical hymns that could, and in many cases have, been set to a wide variety of tunes. Some of his hymns have been set to different tunes in almost every Methodist hymnal in which they have been published, others are part of text-tune pairings that seem unbreakable over longer periods of time, while still others have been set to multiple tunes within the same hymnal. Such variety or stability might be dismissed as of only peripheral historical interest, reflecting changing aesthetic preferences, local customs, or broader traditions, but nonetheless having little impact on the meaning of the hymn, which still resides in the constancy of the text. It is, however, through such changing or stable relationships that hymns acquire much of their meaning for those who encounter them through singing and listening. The familiarity of a well-known tune may carry many different cultural or theological resonances for participants, while aspects of musical style and genre may encourage or inhibit engagement.

Begbie is keen to emphasise that the relationship between words and music is complex, and that influences may flow in both directions.

Strikingly, he challenges the common view that the language of religion divulges its meanings in isolation and more especially that in such isolation 'the more faithfully it will render theological truth'.[15] Rather, he argues, it is vital to consider how the interaction of words with other media, such as music, influences meaning:

> The key question, we suggest, is not whether music (or any other medium) is able to exercise a role vis-à-vis doctrinal discourse, but rather what role it *has* played, *is* playing, and *could* or *should* play.[16]

While Begbie confines himself to discussion of the final part of that question, it is the first and second parts that are most instructive here; the first invites consideration of the ways in which prior musical experiences may have influenced Charles Wesley's hymn writing, and the second shifts the attention to the impact of musical repertoire and practice on worshippers' experience of Charles Wesley's hymns.

Charles Wesley's musical experiences

Charles Wesley experienced a rich variety of musical repertoire and practices in his lifetime. These encompassed music in a range of religious contexts but also music, musicians, and musical events of a secular nature. Music was a regular feature of the Wesley family's devotional life at the rectory in Epworth during Charles's childhood. Describing the ways in which the educational programme implemented by Susanna Wesley for her children overlapped with religious discipline, Charles Wallace notes that 'she adopted the custom of *singing* psalms at the beginning and end of the school day'.[17] Carlton R. Young further notes that the musical life of the parish church in Epworth, where Charles's father, Samuel, was rector, would probably have featured metrical psalmody, especially following the formation of a religious society there in 1702.[18] Whether the 'Old Version' (Sternhold and Hopkins's *The Whole Booke of Psalmes*), the 'New Version' (Tate and Brady's *New Version of the Psalms of David*) or some other metrical psalter was in use in either the parish church or rectory is unknown. While this renders it impossible to identify precise tunes that Charles would have sung, whichever version was used would have exposed him to a musical diet of tunes of largely sixteenth- and seventeenth-century origin in an essentially plain, unadorned style with regular rhythms. Liturgical and devotional singing was thus formational for Charles; the idea that religious truths could be communicated through metrical verse set to music was normative. His subsequent education at Westminster School and Oxford University would have expanded his liturgical musical experiences, notably through the access they provided to the cathedral choral tradition. The singing of his childhood continued into Charles's student days. The regular devotional singing of the Holy Club at Oxford was a contributing factor to the methodical religious lifestyle that gave rise to the initially pejorative appellation 'Methodist'.

In October 1735, Charles and John Wesley set off with several colleagues on board the *Simmonds* for Savannah, Georgia. Although Charles undertook the voyage as private secretary to James Oglethorpe, founder of the Province of Georgia, the whole venture had a distinctly religious emphasis, with John travelling to become minister to the new parish in Savannah, and intent on evangelising Native Americans. The tumultuous voyage, during which the *Simmonds* nearly sank, is principally recounted in terms of its impact on John Wesley, not least because of his vivid account of the storm in his journal. John contrasts the sense of panic among the British voyagers with the serenity of a group of Moravian Christians on board: 'A terrible screaming began among the English. The Germans calmly sung on'.[19] Coupled with John's subsequent efforts to translate German hymns sung by the Moravians and his publication of the *Charleston Hymnal*, properly titled *Psalms and Hymns* (1737), the trip, and the Moravian contact in particular, is deemed to have been highly influential on John in terms of incorporating hymn singing into all aspects of the highly organised societal life that would come to characterise Methodism. Such an emphasis overlooks the potential impact of the trip on Charles. Whether or not he was as impressed as his brother by the Moravian singing on the *Simmonds* is unknown, but he would inevitably have become familiar with the centrality of music to their devotional life and the impact this had on his brother's religious leadership.

These musical influences from Charles's childhood and adulthood can be found in his early outpouring of hymn texts that began in earnest in 1738. The metrical profile of his verse provides the most obvious evidence. Frank Baker argues that his use of metre marks Charles Wesley as a poetic genius, and specifically links this to his musicality:

> Although he could make no great musical claims as a vocalist, instrumentalist, or composer, his musical sons acknowledged that his ear was impeccable. And because there was music in his soul, lilting, rapturous, divine music, he could not be confined to the humdrum in verse.[20]

He goes on to highlight several of the forty-five iambic metres in which Charles was especially prolific, among them Double Short, Double Common, and Double Long metres. Such metrical patterns, especially in their single forms, were the backbone of the metrical psalm tradition with which Charles grew up. That he wrote prolifically in such metres reflects the ingrained musical experience of singing psalms in them, but was not merely a matter of observing convention, for as Baker notes, Charles was also a metrical innovator. Among the metres in which Wesley wrote most prolifically are many not previously strongly associated with English-language hymnody or psalmody. The metre he used most extensively of all was 8.8.8.8.8.8. but he also used many others for smaller numbers of hymns. Baker cites Beckerlegge in suggesting German influence on some of these metres, an assertion that is strengthened when music is taken into consideration.[21] The first Methodist tune-book, commonly known as the *Foundery Collection*, was published in 1742; twenty-eight of its forty-two interlined texts are by Charles Wesley. Twenty-four of its tunes, representing just over half of the total, are in single or double forms of the three metres commonly associated with English metrical psalmody, noted above. Many of these were taken from earlier English sources. The book is notable, however, for including sixteen tunes of Germanic origin. These cover twelve distinct metres, with ten out of the sixteen being in metres other than versions of Short, Common, or Long Metre.[22] These provide evidence not only of the influence of the Moravians on John Wesley but also of the specific influence of Moravian repertoire on Charles Wesley. The tunes represent a sample of repertoire with which he would have become familiar either through his own direct experience of the Moravians, or via his brother's translations of their hymns. In assessing the relationship between Charles Wesley's hymns and music, therefore, it is vital to avoid a trap summarised by Begbie: 'that of assuming these other modes will not have *already* had an impact on the forming and practical use of the primary language'.[23]

Music and Charles Wesley's legacy

'Christ the Lord is risen today'

While the instances above demonstrate the general influence of music on Charles Wesley's hymn writing, there are also occasional instances of a more particular nature. *Hymns and Sacred Poems* (1739) includes Charles's hymn 'Christ the Lord is risen today'. It also appears in the *Foundery Collection*, set to a melody named SALISBURY TUNE, first published in *Lyra Davidica* (1708), a small collection by an anonymous compiler containing translations of German and Latin hymns alongside original English hymns, with tunes interleaved. Wesley's text has its roots in this publication. There, the tune used in the *Foundery Collection* was set to a hymn for Easter, 'Jesus Christ is risen today' and a translation of the German Easter hymn 'Erstanden ist der Heilige Christ', the first line of which is 'Christ our Lord is Risen today'. Wesley places his opening line in quotation marks, showing his indebtedness to the earlier hymns.[24]

Figure 1: SALISBURY TUNE from *Foundery Collection* (1742)

Wesley's opening line is closer to the opening of the translated German hymn, but thereafter, neither of the earlier hymns serves as a close model; rather, as Neil Dixon notes, he draws on a wide range of biblical and other literary sources.[25] Whether Wesley was responding to one or both of these texts is arguably less significant than that he was responding to the melody. The setting of his new Easter hymn to it in the *Foundery Collection* strongly suggests that it was not just the Easter lyrics that had inspired Wesley, but that their association with an exuberant tune appealed to him in terms of capturing the meaning of the resurrection. In Begbie's terms, this might seem closest to conformance, a pairing of words and music considered 'successful just to the extent that the media align, accord with each other'.[26] Yet the tune is associated with three Easter texts, each of which is unique: 'Jesus Christ is risen today' is a simple hymn of praise; the translation of 'Erstanden ist der Heilige Christ' is a narrative, incorporating a dialogue between the Angel and Mary at the tomb; Wesley's eleven stanzas are a theological reflection on the resurrection and the promise of salvation. While the tune may seem appropriate to each, they do not conform with it in the same ways. Rather, as Begbie indicates, following Cook, the media cohere in fruitful ways: 'they elaborate *in different ways* some "third" reality, an underlying content, idea, scene, emotion, or whatever'.[27] It would seem to be this relationship to which Wesley responded in his own text, perceiving the tune through its existing association as suitable for capturing the joy of Easter, but also offering the potential to express that anew in partnership with his own words; as Begbie puts it, 'The music is *appropriate* to the text but appropriate *in musical ways*.'[28]

While the identification of precise textual and musical inspiration for 'Christ the Lord is risen today' is unusual in terms of Wesley's overall output, more unusual still is the longevity of the relationship between the words and tune. Since 1742, the relationship has been maintained throughout Methodism's history; the current authorised Methodist hymnals in Great Britain and the USA preserve the pairing. It is more common for texts by Charles Wesley that remain in use to have been paired with many different tunes since the eighteenth century. A case study focused on another of his most famous hymns, 'O for a thousand tongues to sing', exemplifies the ways in which different musical settings of the same text affect the relationship between words and music and provides insight into Charles Wesley's musical legacy.

'O for a thousand tongues to sing'

'O for a thousand tongues to sing' can be regarded as the signature hymn of Methodism, owing to its place as the first hymn in the 1780 *Collection*, a positioning replicated in many later Methodist hymnals. It is an extract of a longer hymn, 'Glory to God, and praise, and love', first published in *Hymns and Sacred Poems* (1740); the practice of using

'O for a thousand tongues to sing' as the opening stanza of a hymn dates back to John Wesley's *Hymns and Spiritual Songs* (1753). Despite its prominent status, there has been very little consistency in the tunes associated with it in British Methodism, whereas in the USA, it has become firmly wedded to the tune AZMON. As a Common Metre text, the choice of tunes is vast, and it is notable that those paired with it in British Methodist hymnals since the eighteenth century have varied markedly in character.

In the fifth edition of *A Collection of Hymns for the Use of the People Called Methodists* (1786), a tune name was appended to each hymn. For this hymn, the tune was BIRSTALL, which, like virtually all the indicated tunes, was to be found in *Sacred Harmony* (1781), the final collection of hymn tunes issued under John Wesley's authority, where it is labelled BURSTAL. The tune's earliest publication was in *Sacred Melody* (1761), an earlier Methodist tune book, and its origins are unknown. It is also specified for two other hymns, emphasising that at this stage in the development of hymnody, fixed and unique pairings of words and music were not customary. The tune itself is characterised by much use of melisma, generally short in length. Unlike later tunes associated with this text, it is in the minor mode. While the melody is attractive, there is no obvious way in which it offers the unitary conformance that Begbie suggests has long been the idealised relationship between words and music in religious contexts; there is no reason to regard it as anything more than a functional, accessible tune in the correct metre (see Figure 2).

Between 1786 and the mid nineteenth century, no single tune emerged as the standard, but amid the variety of musical settings, a common characteristic emerges. Tunes that extended the basic Common Metre by requiring the repetition of one or more lines of each stanza were frequently set to Wesley's text. They sometimes included short polyphonic passages, typically in conjunction with the textual repetitions. An early example of such a tune associated with this hymn is OLDHAM, composed by James Leach of Rochdale and first published in *A New Sett of Hymns and Psalm Tunes* (1789). Typical of many such publications of this period, Leach's collection sought to serve the musical needs of a range of Christian traditions rather than being firmly connected with a particular denomination. There is evidence that such tunes were sung by Methodists; two mid-nineteenth-century volumes published for the use of Wesleyan congregations set 'O for a thousand tongues to sing'

Figure 2: BURSTAL from *Sacred Harmony* (1781)

to different tunes of this type. The tune WILTSHIRE appears in the *Companion to the Wesleyan Hymnbook* (1847) and FANCY in Booth's *Wesleyan Psalmist* (1857).

In terms of the influence of music on Charles Wesley's legacy, what matters here is not the specific tunes but the emergence of a type of tune that would be regarded as typically Methodist, for which Percy Scholes coined the term 'Old Methodist'.[29] The quantity of these tunes published in the early nineteenth century indicates that they had supplanted other tune types such as metrical psalm tunes and Germanic melodies found in eighteenth-century Methodist collections. Their uncomplicated melodic, rhythmic and harmonic character and textual repetitions give them an emphatic quality that gave rise to the spirited singing for which Methodists were widely known. Singing them to 'O for a thousand tongues to sing' or other hymn texts by Charles Wesley brought words and music together in an identifiably Methodist way. While there is no evidence to suggest that 'O for a thousand tongues to

Music and Charles Wesley's legacy

Figure 3: WILTSHIRE from *Companion to the Wesleyan Hymnbook* (1847)

sing' was unusually highly regarded prior to 1780, its position as the first hymn in John Wesley's 'Large Hymn Book' meant that it rapidly acquired extra significance, either as later compilers only supplemented Wesley's hymnal or because they retained this hymn's placement in their own work. While it may be fanciful to interpret the polyphonic sections of some of these tunes as giving musical expression to the text's 'thousand

69

tongues', this musical characteristic, along with the repetition of lines, conspicuously draws attention to the act of singing. The text makes its own contribution in terms of the hymn's meaningfulness as an expression of Methodism's distinctive beliefs and practices, notably its fusing of themes of praise, evangelism, forgiveness, healing, assurance and salvation. Tunes such as Leach's make their own contribution too, and do so, in Begbie's terms, in musical ways. In drawing attention to the act of singing, they resonate with early Methodism's emphasis on the shared exercise of religious faith and the importance of individual participation within a communal context, explicitly including in song, as cogently expressed in John Wesley's 'Directions for Singing'.[30]

The late nineteenth century and early twentieth century saw a marked change in the musical settings of 'O for a thousand tongues to sing', as well as the adoption of the text, along with others by Charles Wesley, in Anglican hymnals. A more general change in the publication of hymnals is also important to note in this period; the earlier practice of separate books of texts and tunes was gradually replaced by single-volume publications that provided a fixed tune for every text. In many cases, this consolidated specific relationships between texts and tunes, although no such consensus is evident in the case of 'O for a thousand tongues to sing'. The hymnals of the two largest nineteenth-century Methodist bodies, the Wesleyan Connexion and the Primitive Methodist Connexion both print tunes of a more restrained character for this hymn than those described above. *Wesley's Hymns and New Supplement*, an expanded edition of the 1780 *Collection* published by the Wesleyans in 1876 retains 'O for a thousand tongues to sing' as the first hymn and sets it to WINCHESTER OLD, first published in Thomas Este's *The Whole Booke of Psalmes* (1592). *The Primitive Methodist Hymnal* (1889), meanwhile, employs the tune MANCHESTER, composed by Robert Wainwright (1748–82). Although Wainwright's tune makes much use of melisma, neither it nor WINCHESTER OLD extend the basic Common Metre; the latter in particular is typical of its type in its narrow melodic range and plain, regular rhythms.

According to the Methodist hymnologist James T. Lightwood, WINCHESTER OLD's selection in the Wesleyan hymnal was due to its musical editor Henry J. Gauntlett, who rejected the hymnal committee's original choice of Thomas Haweis's RICHMOND.[31] Gauntlett was a respected organist and church musician, whose appointment as musical editor rested on his musical reputation rather than any prior association with Methodism. The musical editor of *The Primitive Methodist Hymnal*, Henry Coward, had a similar pedigree as a choral director and musical educator. That Gauntlett's intervention was accepted by the Wesleyan committee accords with the musical character of the 1876 hymnal more broadly. Along with *The Primitive Methodist Hymnal* and other Methodist publications in this period, it was heavily influenced by the recent success of the *Hymns Ancient and Modern* (1861; second edition, 1875), the first hymnal to gain widespread popularity across the Church of England. It was part of a broader shift towards greater professionalisation and standardisation of parochial church music, as organs and choirs became commonplace. Although Methodism had been formally separated from the Church of England for decades, its musical practices and repertoire show the clear influence of Anglicanism, reflecting a desire to match it in terms of fashion and respectability. Here, musical choices such as WINCHESTER OLD and MANCHESTER alter the meanings associated with 'O for a thousand tongues to sing'. While the textual themes remain constant, singing the words to such tunes reins in the exuberance that might have been associated with the performance of the earlier tunes, conveying instead a sense of late-nineteenth-century Methodist respectability.

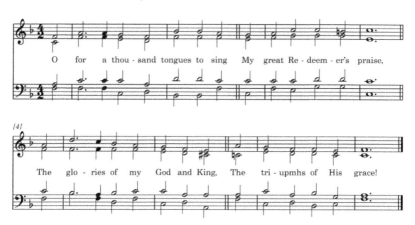

Figure 4: WINCHESTER OLD from *The Methodist Hymn Book* (1904)

This trend continued into the early twentieth century, as WINCHESTER OLD was retained in *The Methodist Hymn Book* (1904), a joint publication of the Wesleyan Connexion and the Methodist New

Connexion. Whether a hymnal's musical selections reflect the widespread preferences of the denomination it seeks to serve or merely the views of those in positions of institutional authority as compilers and editors is impossible to ascertain conclusively; the printed record preserves and therefore likely privileges the latter, whereas details of the tunes sung week-by-week in local chapels are not recorded. Evidence from successive hymnals may, however, be cautiously used to identify possible tensions and compromises between institutional preferences and popular demand.

The Methodist Hymn Book (1933) was published one year after Methodist reunification and sets two tunes to 'O for a thousand tongues to sing', which retains its place as the first hymn. Haweis's RICHMOND, rejected by Gauntlett, finds favour, while LYDIA, attributed to Thomas Phillips is the second tune.[32] The tunes contrast each other in numerous ways. Haweis's triple-time RICHMOND has an elegant, expansive melody, with a striking opening arpeggio and a climactic sequential third phrase, whereas LYDIA is in quadruple time, derives its melodic interest from scalic passages, and achieves a climax through its extension of the basic metrical pattern, requiring the final line of each stanza to be repeated. Though possibly later than Haweis's tune, it has a more rustic character, redolent of the enthusiastic singing of the early Methodists, as reflected in two references to it in nineteenth-century fiction.[33] Vigorous tunes of late-eighteenth- or early-nineteenth-century origin such as LYDIA and Thomas Jarman's LYNGHAM, considered below, were not entirely absent from the late-nineteenth-century hymnals discussed

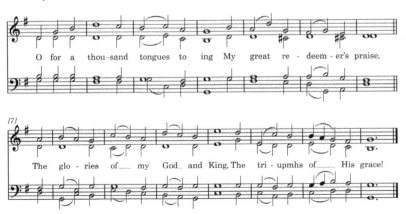

Figure 5: RICHMOND from *The Methodist Hymn Book* (1933)

above. Rather, they were usually included without texts in appendices of supplemental tunes. In some instances, such as *The Methodist Hymn Book* (1904), the preface makes clear that the appendix is a concession to popular taste and that its contents did not meet with the approval of esteemed musical editors.[34]

In *Hymns and Psalms* (1983), LYDIA was appointed as the first set tune for 'O for a thousand tongues to sing', with RICHMOND moved to the second tune.[35] Its successor, *Singing the Faith* (2011), retains LYDIA, drops RICHMOND, and adds LYNGHAM as a second tune. Though never before set to these words in an authorised Methodist hymnal, LYNGHAM is routinely found in appendices of supplemental tunes. Although set as an alternative to 'While shepherds watched their flocks by night' in *Hymns and Psalms*, J. R. Watson and Kenneth Trickett observe that 'it has also frequently been set to "O for a thousand tongues to sing" and "Come, let us join our cheerful songs"'.[36] This is further suggested by its pairing with these words in three non-denominational hymnals in the late twentieth century: *Songs and Hymns of Fellowship* (1987), *Let's Praise* (1988) and *Mission Praise* (1990).

Figure 6: LYDIA from *Hymns and Psalms* (1983)

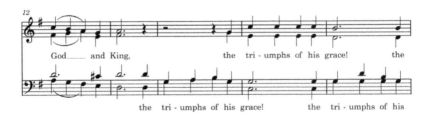
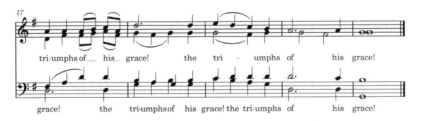

Figure 7: LYNGHAM from *Singing the Faith* (2011)

The meanings brought about by these pairings might seem to be consistent with those generated by the use of similar tunes noted above. Additionally, however, these tunes convey a strong sense of Methodist heritage that would not have been the case when they were first written and sung. A concern with Methodism's custodianship of Charles Wesley's hymns was especially apparent in the preparation of *Hymns and Psalms*. Faced with a very large body of material written since the 1933 hymnal, the number of Wesley's hymns was inevitably considerably reduced as draft contents lists were prepared. This led to the passing of a motion at the Methodist Conference in 1980 that the hymnal should contain at least two hundred hymns by Charles Wesley. Although this target was not in fact met in the final publication, Watson and Trickett argue that it was nonetheless critical in ensuring the Conference's approval of the project as a whole.[37] The round number, which would have accounted for approximately one quarter of the hymns in the book, indicates the contested legacy of Charles Wesley's hymns; for some, the fact of their authorship demanded their inclusion in substantial numbers, while the mandating of this reveals that this was not a uniformly accepted position. In a period marked by ecumenical opportunities and tensions, ideas about Methodist heritage and identity were naturally foregrounded. Alongside the volume of Charles Wesley's texts, as resolved in 1980, the greater prominence given to tunes such as LYDIA and LYNGHAM can be seen as part of this broader concern. They draw out meanings that are not present in the text itself but only implicit in its historical status. Though not necessarily the actual tunes to which this text was sung in early Methodism, they emphasise Methodist distinctiveness and in their vitality prompt collective recall of key tropes of Methodist history concerning its energetic evangelism and lively worship, of which 'O for a thousand tongues to sing' is especially emblematic given its historic positioning in the denomination's hymnals.

Although the hymn has featured in many Anglican hymnals since *Hymns Ancient and Modern*, these have generally employed different musical settings from those found in Methodism. Absent are the lively, extended tunes and in their place are a range of more restrained Common Metre tunes. The tune SELBY, for example, was set to the hymn in the second edition of *Hymns Ancient and Modern* and continued to be associated with it in many hymnals belonging to that series, including *Common Praise* (2000). *Ancient and Modern: Hymns and Songs for Refreshing Worship* (2013), however, departed significantly from this pattern. It included two tunes: RICHMOND, which had some prior Anglican association with these words, and LYNGHAM. The latter suggests a desire on the part of the editors to encourage Anglican congregations to benefit not only from Charles Wesley's words, to which they have long had access, but also from a style of tune and associated manner of singing that has been considered distinctively Methodist. This is a clear instance of music bringing its own meaning in musical ways to this hymn; value is accorded to words and music both separately and in partnership.

'O for a thousand tongues' reflects in a potent way the importance of music in Charles Wesley's legacy. Remaining one of his most widely sung hymns, its association with a wide range of tunes has enabled music to shape its meanings in musical ways for different congregations, times and contexts.

Original musical settings of Charles Wesley's hymns

None of the hymn tunes discussed so far were originally composed for the words by Charles Wesley with which they have been paired. Brief consideration of musical settings that were composed for that purpose highlights other ways in which Charles Wesley's legacy has been shaped by music. Among John and Charles Wesley's wide circle of acquaintances and followers were members of London's theatrical community, including musicians. The German-born J. F. Lampe was among the most prominent, and in 1746 he published original settings of Charles's hymn texts as *Twenty Four Hymns on the Great Festivals and Other Occasions*. These apparently came to the attention of Handel, who composed his own settings to three of the twenty-four texts. In 1765, Jonathan Battishill, a noted church and theatre musician, composed a set of *Twelve Hymns, the Words by the Rev. Mr. Charles Wesley*. All three wrote for solo voices with keyboard accompaniment in a fashionable idiom influenced by stage music. Although the Wesleys enthusiastically adopted Lampe's tunes for congregational use, such secular influences were frowned upon by others, suggesting the contest model of the relationship outlined by Begbie.[38] As he notes, contest between words and music has been a particular source of Protestant anxiety, yet noting Cook's observation that some element of contest is always present in multimedia relationships, he goes on to suggest that 'the interaction of incompatible elements can result in a richer perception of whatever the text is engaging or making accessible'.[39] For their initial audiences, these settings would likely have emphasised the contrast between the subject matter of Wesley's words and the lyrical content more usually associated with music composed in such a familiar style. The apparent success of Methodism's engagement with London's theatrical community suggests that such musical contest was fruitful.[40]

Twentieth-century Methodist hymnals provide evidence of attempts to overcome a perceived contest between words and music in Charles Wesley's 'And can it be that I should gain'. Written shortly after his conversion experience in 1738, it subsequently became strongly associated with the tune SAGINA, a striking example of the 'Old Methodist' type of tune. Successive hymnal committees clearly found the relationship between Wesley's words of wonder at God's grace and the rambunctious tune incongruous.[41] G. C. Martin's HOLY FAITH (1904), Alfred Beer's LANSDOWN (1933) and Cyril V. Taylor's DIDSBURY (1983) were all commissioned as alternatives. That none of them survived in conjunction with Wesley's text in successor hymnals indicates that congregations were more accepting of the contest between the words and SAGINA, or even did not perceive it.[42]

In the twenty-first century, a small number of Charles Wesley's hymn texts have received new musical settings from solo artists and groups in idioms associated with the Contemporary Christian worship music genre. Nathan Fellingham and Phatfish's 2011 setting of 'And can it be' exemplifies this development. Music plays an important role in the meaning of such versions. The powerful message of Wesley's words is a crucial factor; for them to retain devotional value in contemporary Christian worship, it appears necessary to replace the traditional musical idiom with one much more familiar to worshippers used to band-led worship music. However, the prior influence of earlier musical repertoire on such new settings should not be overlooked or underestimated; it is inconceivable that a band such as Phatfish, immersed in British evangelicalism, would have encountered the words separately from their association with SAGINA. Thus, even though the desire to make use of a completely different musical idiom remains important, the role of music in arriving at this point must be acknowledged. Indeed, Fellingham's repetition of the final couplet in each stanza suggests a direct influence, matching the same repetition found in SAGINA.

Charles Wesley, music and Methodism

Charles Wesley's own musical experiences, the tunes in many different musical styles set to his words, and the original creative responses of musicians to his texts from the eighteenth to the twenty-first century all demonstrate the importance of music in understanding his legacy. Music influenced his poetic work in multiple ways, shaping how and what he wrote. It was central to his formative disciplines of prayer, study and devotion, which in turn shaped his copious provision of hymns for eighteenth-century Methodist life. The musical qualities of different tunes imparted meanings to him and in turn informed the meanings associated with his hymns in subsequent generations. Composers have found musical challenge and opportunity in Charles Wesley's work, drawing on Methodism's musical heritage as well as responding to textual meanings.

Returning to Campbell's theoretical framework for Methodist historiography, it remains clear that Charles Wesley's hymns form a strong part of Methodist foundational narratives. Campbell's approach is text focused, however, and does not consider the meanings that music has added to the texts as they have been sung by subsequent generations, and the impact this had on making them prominent in histories of Methodism. Some such histories do emphasise the practice of singing and it would thus seem appropriate to expand Campbell's framework to include a narrative module focused on hymn singing. This would acknowledge that singing was commonly identified a central part of early Methodist practice and that there were bilateral influences between music and Charles Wesley's hymnody.

Begbie's theological adaptation of Cook's theory of multimedia relationships emerges as a fruitful framework for understanding the historical significance of music in congregational song. The different ways in which Charles Wesley's hymns have influenced and been influenced by music add weight to Begbie's proposition that, in religious-musical contexts, text might assume primacy:

> It is surely quite possible to hold that a text, say, should take the semantic lead, that there should be a primary or guiding concern to be faithful to the semantic constraints and direction of a given text, while at the same time believing that music can interact with that text in our perception of it so as to enable a fuller and deeper engagement with the realities with which that text deals, and in this sense to provoke or elicit new and fresh meanings.[43]

Begbie is primarily concerned with music's potential to influence theological insight. Consideration of the range of meanings that different musical settings have had on Charles Wesley's hymn texts, however, demonstrate that his model has broader applicability. Musical meanings may draw attention to devotional, cultural, social and historical factors that are only secondarily connected to the 'realities with which that text deals', yet they nonetheless add much to the significance worshippers attach to hymns, which can be understood in both content and practice as instances of what Astley terms 'ordinary theology'.[44] The centrality of hymns to Charles Wesley's legacy owes much to their association with music, through which his texts have been experienced and interpreted, and by which their meanings and value have been shaped.

Notes

[1] See P. Olleson, 'Charles Wesley and his Children', in K. G. C. Newport and T. A. Campbell (eds), *Charles Wesley: Life, literature and legacy* (Peterborough, 2007).

[2] J. E. Rattenbury, *The Eucharistic Hymns of John and Charles Wesley* (London, 1948).

[3] J. E. Rattenbury, *The Evangelical Doctrines of Charles Wesley's Hymns* (London, 1941).

[4] For example, D. B. Stevick, *The Altar's Fire: Charles Wesley's Hymns on the Lord's Supper* (Peterborough, 2004); J. A. Lunn, *The Theology of Resignation and Sanctification in Charles Wesley's Hymns* (Abingdon, 2019).

[5] T. A. Campbell, *Encoding Methodism: Telling and retelling narratives of Wesleyan origins* (Nashville TN, 2017), p. 10.

[6] Campbell, *Encoding Methodism*, p. 15.

[7] D. Hempton, *Methodism: Empire of the Spirit* (New Haven, 2005), pp. 72–3.

[8] Methodist Conference, *The Methodist Hymn Book* (London, 1933), p. iii.

[9] Hempton, *Methodism*, p. 73.

[10] J. Begbie, *Music, Modernity and God: Essays in listening* (Oxford, 2013), p. 180. Begbie makes particular use of N. Cook, *Analysing Musical Multimedia* (Oxford, 1994).

[11] Begbie, *Music, Modernity and God*, p. 181.

[12] J. Wesley, 'Thoughts on the Power of Music', in *The Arminian Magazine*, vol. 4 (1781), 103–7.

[13] Journal entry for 6 April 1781, Bicentennial Edition of *The Works of John Wesley*, general editors Frank Baker, Richard P. Heitzenrater, and Randy L. Maddox (Oxford, 1975–83, and Nashville: Abingdon Press, 1984–) [henceforth identified as *Works*, followed by volume and page numbers], 23:198. Here, he aligns with, in Begbie's words, 'practically every theorist of church music who has addressed music-word relations'. *Music, Modernity and God*, p. 182.

[14] Begbie, *Music, Modernity and God*, p. 182.

[15] Ibid., p. 204.

[16] Ibid., p. 204.

[17] C. Wallace, 'Charles Wesley and Susanna', in Newport and Campbell, *Charles Wesley: Life, literature and legacy*, p. 74.

[18] C. R. Young, 'The Musical Charles Wesley' in Newport and Campbell, *Charles Wesley: Life, literature and legacy*, pp. 415, 438–9, n14.

[19] Journal entry for 25 January 1735, *Works*, 18:143.

20   F. Baker, *Representative Verse of Charles Wesley, Selected and Edited with an Introduction* (London, 1962), p. xliv.

21   Baker, *Representative Verse*, pp. xlv–xlvii.

22   See M. V. Clarke, 'John Wesley and Methodist Music in the Eighteenth Century: Principles and Practice', University of Durham PhD thesis, 2008, pp. 155–67.

23   Begbie, *Music, Modernity and God*, p. 204.

24   N. Dixon, 'Christ the Lord is risen today', in *The Canterbury Dictionary of Hymnology*, http://www.hymnology.co.uk/c/christ-the-lord-is-risen-today (accessed 27 January 2024).

25   Dixon, 'Christ the Lord is risen today'.

26   Begbie, *Music, Modernity and God*, p. 180.

27   Ibid., p. 183.

28   Ibid., p. 183.

29   P. A. Scholes, *The Oxford Companion to Music*, Tenth Edition (London, 1970), p. 631.

30   See M. V. Clarke, 'John Wesley's "Direction for Singing": Methodist hymnody as an expression of Methodist beliefs in thought and practice', in *Methodist History*, vol. 47, no. 4 (2009), 196–209.

31   J. T. Lightwood, *The Music of the Methodist Hymn-Book, Being the Story of Each Tune With Biographical Notices of the Composers* (London, 1935), p. 2.

32   Evidence that RICHMOND may well have been sung to this text despite Gauntlett's objections can be found in the Anglican *English Hymnal* (1906), where although a tune named O GOD OF LOVE is printed with the text, RICHMOND is identified as an alternative.

33   Lightwood, *Music of the Methodist Hymn-Book*, p. 3.

34   M. V. Clarke, *British Methodist Hymnody: Theology, Heritage, and Experience* (Abingdon, 2018), p. 128.

35   A third tune, UNIVERSITY, is added, reflecting the hymnal's aim to be, in the words of its original subtitle, 'a Methodist and Ecumenical Hymn Book', given its association with these words in hymnals for Congregational churches. R. Watson and K. Trickett (eds), *Companion to Hymns and Psalms* (Peterborough, 1988), p. 424.

36   Watson and Trickett, *Companion*, p. 103. Ironically, its inclusion with this Christmas carol places it alongside WINCHESTER OLD.

37   Watson and Trickett, *Companion*, p. 1.

38   T. Jackson (ed.), *The Journal of The Rev. Charles Wesley*, vol. 2 (London, 1849), p. 174.

39   Begbie, *Music, Modernity and God*, p. 212.

40   See M. V. Clarke, 'Charles Wesley, Methodism and New Art Music in the Long Eighteenth Century' in *Eighteenth-Century Music*, vol. 18, no. 2 (2021).

41   P. Westermeyer, *Let the People Sing: Hymn Tunes in Perspective* (Chicago, 2005), p. 199.

42   See M. V. Clarke, '"And can it be": Analysing the Words, Music, and Contexts of an Iconic Methodist Hymn' in *Yale Journal of Music and Religion*, vol. 2, no. 1 (2016), 25–52, for a detailed discussion of this hymn and its musical settings.

43   Begbie, *Music, Modernity and God*, p. 191.

44   J. Astley, *Ordinary Theology: Looking, Listening and Learning in Theology* (Aldershot, 2002).

PORTRAITS OF CHARLES WESLEY (1707–88)

Peter S. Forsaith

This contribution explains how Charles Wesley has been portrayed visually in his lifetime and later. It notes the paradox that 'Charles Wesley, who moved in cultural and artistic circles, should have so few portraits compared to his brother John, who eschewed such company.' While there are contemporary portraits at least ostensibly from the life, his posthumous portrayals have typically been in heroic style, celebrating one of the founding fathers of Methodism.

Keywords: Charles Wesley, portraits, art, iconography, Methodism

Introduction

It seems perverse that Charles Wesley, who moved in cultural and artistic circles, should have so few portraits compared to his brother John, who eschewed such company.[1] Charles Wesley was a poet, his sons musicians, so, especially after they moved to London around 1771, were in touch with the cultural life of the capital, as is evidenced by the attendance at the boys' subscription concerts. Yet there is only a handful of images of Charles, either 'from the life' or posthumous, whereas those of John are legion.

Elsewhere I have suggested that the two splendid half-length portraits of his sons Charles and Samuel, by John Russell RA, which today hang in the Royal Academy of Music in London (a short walk from where Charles Wesley and family once lived), were painted as something of showpieces, maybe for Russell's studio; or that they hung in their home where they gave their 'subscription concerts'.[2] These alone indicate that the Charles Wesley family were no strangers to art.

https://doi.org/10.16922/jrhlc.10.2.6

What is also known is that in the early 1820s, when James Everett visited the Marylebone house, he 'was ushered into a room hung round with family portraits', though he gave no further detail.[3] Thomas Jackson similarly attested to there being a family collection around that time.[4] By 1839, Charles, Sally and Samuel were all dead but it seems that the pictures may have passed to a Mrs Green, a relative on the Gwynne side, who had cared for Charles junior after Sally had died, and was his executor.[5]

She then offered a number of pictures to the Wesleyan church, including one of 'Rev. C. Wesley, shorter length, life size' for which she asked 70 guineas. The year 1839 was celebrated as the 'Wesleyan centenary': Wesley's first Methodist society was formed in 1739, when John Wesley also commenced his public evangelistic ministry. There was then a growing interest in historic portraits; further, the new Wesleyan headquarters building in Bishopsgate, London, had blank walls which might be used for pictures to illuminate its past. Only two of the pictures offered were then acquired, including the one mentioned of Charles Wesley – which was possibly that by John Russell (although conceivably could be the 'Lily Portrait').

Mrs Green also had several other Wesley family portraits which she did not then offer. Whether any of the pictures then passed into institutional or individual Methodist ownership at her death in 1856 is unknown, but might not be unlikely. By the early Victorian period, the last of the generation of those who could remember the Wesley brothers, and might possess portraits or items associated with them, were dying and their possessions disposed of. Equally, there was also a growing interest among Methodists in acquiring material relating to the past. The 'connexion' of Methodist religious societies John Wesley and his brother had developed had metamorphosed into a separate nonconformist denomination, which was developing a foundational narrative around its originators, although one in which Charles Wesley had a very secondary place. It was a time when, under a young queen and her energetic consort, it felt like a new age.

However, very few portraits of John Wesley have a history prior to the mid-nineteenth century while, as will become clear, the provenance of any of those of Charles Wesley cannot be traced clearly before about 1900. This iconography is therefore offered with the caveat that further research and the passage of time may well bring fresh material to light and render what follows as inaccurate or incomplete. Like a portrait, it is a snapshot which is taken in a particular time and place.

Thanks are owed to staff at those places which have portraits of Charles Wesley for kindly supplying a variety of details about their pictures in response to my questions. Without them this work would not have been possible.

Abbreviations

JRRILM	Archives of the Methodist Church, John Rylands Research Institute and Library, University of Manchester.
NPG	National Portrait Gallery, London.
WHS	Wesley Historical Society Library, Oxford.
H/S	Head and shoulders
H/L	Half-length
TQL	Three-quarter length
o/c	Oils on canvas
Prot.	Prototype [original work]
Prov.	Provenance (previous history)
Exhib.	Exhibition
Exmpls.	Examples
Deriv.	Derived from another image.

Notes

Unless otherwise stated, all dimensions are height × width.

Painted Portraits from the Life

ANON.

notes.   Pair of miniatures attributed as of John and Charles Wesley as young men, possibly when at Oxford.

prot.   John Wesley's House and Museum of Methodism, City Road, [LDWMM2006/10418/1–2] possibly oils on ivory (each) 3.5 × 2.5 cm.

Note accompanies: 'the Wesley brothers as young men'. While the costume might suggest a later date than 1720s–1730s, the physiognomic likenesses are closely related to John and Charles given that while Charles Wesley later wore a wig for all other known portraits, he had his own hair when younger. An alternative identification as Charles Wesley's sons Charles and Samuel is unlikely. They were discovered in 1917 stored with the will of Martha Wesley, which suggests provenance within the family.[6]

ANON. (The 'Lily Portrait')

notes. Although probably the best known and most reproduced painting of Charles Wesley, there is no firm evidence that this very appealing work of art is actually of him. The picture hung in the Wesleyan Book Room boardroom in London by 1907 but its previous history is unknown.[7] It may possibly have been in the family, then passed with other pictures to Mrs Green, as suggested earlier; maybe the 'shorter length, life size'. While the identification as Charles Wesley has never been questioned, this might be reinforced by a physiognomic facial comparison with John Russell's portrait of Charles's eponymous son.[8] That might then be extended to include a portrait supposedly of his father, Rev. Samuel Wesley (1661–1735) which has come to light in recent years.[9] But it would be unwise to put overmuch weight on these.

Nor is it easy to date the picture. The youthful face would suggest a man in his twenties. The lilies depicted suggest purity (and did not then connote marriage), so might refer to Charles Wesley's ordinations in 1735. Further, the pose reflects the portrait just mentioned, putatively of his father, who died months before Charles Wesley was ordained. However, this is the realm of supposition. Alternately, the lilies might simply be a punning visual homage to the portraitist Sir Peter Lely (1618–80): this portrait has something of Lely's style about it.

There is further symbolism in the painting: a clergy wig and preaching bands indicate an ordained clergyman. The right hand holding a book suggests a clergyman or scholar (Charles Wesley was both) while the left hand splayed across the heart indicates piety.

Various names have been suggested as the artist, most notably Thomas Hudson (1701–79). While there might be some slight comparability with elements of Hudson's style, this is evidently a fanciful attribution: there is no direct evidence such as a signature to link it to Hudson.[10] The peripatetic minor portraitist John Michael Williams (1710–c.1780) painted both Mrs Wesley (1737) and John Wesley (c.1743); it is not beyond possibility that this is by him but again, there is no evidence. Both Hudson and Williams were influenced by Jonathan

Richardson (1667–1745), an influence which may be seen in this picture. Often the publication of a contemporary print from a portrait enables a definite attribution to the artist: there is no such derivative print here.

In conclusion, while this portrait is not positively identified as being of Charles Wesley, nor artist nor date known, there seems no compelling reason to dispute its identification as of him, nor is a dating to mid-1730s unlikely.

prot.   John Wesley's Chapel (The 'New Room'), The Horsefair, Bristol, [work located in Charles Wesley's House, 5, Charles St, Bristol]; oils on canvas 92.7 × 72.4 cm. TQL facing L, R hand holding book, L hand splayed across chest. Clerical bands and wig. Plain ground, spray of lilies in foreground.

Prov.:   Wesleyan Book Room to Wesley's Chapel, London, thence to Epworth Old Rectory, Epworth, Lincs. Transferred to Charles Wesley's House, Bristol, May 2018.

copies   [see below] Richard Gilmore DOUGLAS (*c.*1937–), Charles Wesley's House, Charles St, Bristol. NR2011.41, acrylic on canvas, 90.0 × 59.7 cm. Richard Douglas is an artist and retired art teacher who was a volunteer at Epworth Old Rectory.

John RUSSELL RA (1745–1806)   1771

notes.   After the removal of Charles Wesley's family to London in 1771, John Russell painted members of the family, as well as John Wesley.[11] Alongside his striking *c.*1770s portrait of Sarah Gwynne/Wesley, a portrait of her in old age and wearing Welsh traditional clothes is attributed to him. His full-lengths of Charles junior and Samuel junior survive, that of Sally is now unknown, although it was possibly the image of her used by Marshall Claxton in his large picture of John Wesley's deathbed, 'Holy Triumph'.[12]

Russell was then a rising young artist, but his evangelical conversion in 1764 negatively affected his career as he tended to inflict his religious zeal upon his clients. He did, though, paint several leading Methodists including Rev. Martin Madan and his wife (1771), Lady Huntingdon

(1773), and George Whitefield (1768); also the young William Wilberforce, then aged eleven (1770).

Although his portraits of the Wesley family are in oils, Russell is best known for his portraits in pastels. Apprenticed to Francis Cotes, he developed his own style and published *Elements of Painting with Crayons* in 1772 which became an influential treatise on the subject.[13] He was elected a Royal Academician in 1788 and was appointed painter to the King the following year.

prot.   John Wesley's House and Museum of Methodism, London, LDWMM/1997/6656, oils on canvas 80 × 64 cm. HL, facing L, seated, holding book upright in R hand. Plain dark ground.

exhib.   3rd National Portrait Exhibition, 1868 (photo in catalogue).

copies   Richard Gilmore DOUGLAS (*c.*1937–) q.v., two versions:

Charles Wesley's House, Charles St., Bristol NR2011.030, oil on hardboard, 40.8 × 30.5 cm.

Epworth Old Rectory, Epworth, Lincs., EPWOR 2009-306, oil on board, 40.8 × 30.5 cm.

engrv.   T. A. DEAN (1801–60)
n.d., line, 127 × 94 cm. 'From and Original Painting in the possession of the Family' which indicates a date prior to 1834, or that it was then owned by Mrs Green. 'T.A. Dean was a line and stipple engraver who was active in London, exhibiting his work at the Royal Academy and at the Suffolk Street Gallery between 1773 and 1825.'[14] This is probably *c.*1830s–40s. There is an apparently identical, slightly smaller, print inscr. 'Dick. sc.' (105 × 89 cm).

Sarah WESLEY (1759–1828) and
Charles WESLEY junior (1757–1834)   *c.*1776
'Revd. Charles Wesley coming from preaching'

notes.   Sally Wesley visited John Russell's family at Guildford and possibly received drawing lessons from him.[15] This coloured caricature depicts Charles Wesley coming from preaching in the square, presumably

Portraits of Charles Wesley (1707–88)

St James Square, Kingsdown, Bristol, close by the family home in Charles Street.[16] Wesley is being introduced to a number of colliers. The figures are numbered, against them Sally Wesley, herself colourfully dressed, has put acerbic comments as an 'Explanation'. Of herself; 'The Rev. C.W.'s daughter . . . who stands patiently by while her dear papa shakes hands with *all* the colliers, not knowing that she must do so too. A perfect pattern. Dear lady!' Behind her 'Some Methodist sisters lamenting the vanity of dress in Miss W.'

Inscr. 'From a Pen and Ink Sketch by Miss Wesley, daughter of Rev. C. Wesley & her Brother C. Wesley Jr.'

prot. Two copies at JRRILM: DDWES 1/62 [draft], 1/62A.

ANON.   *c.*1780s

notes. Full length side view, wearing long coat with large collar. Clergy wig, carries [tricorn] hat and stick. Pastels, unsigned. Any previous history prior to the picture being given to Trewint Cottage, Cornwall *c.*1950 is unknown. It is presumed to be of Charles Wesley; which the clergy wig reinforces.

The coat may be the top coat referred to by James Everett when visiting the Wesleys' family home in Marylebone in December 1822. This had been stolen from the house a few days before, about which Charles Wesley junior was very upset: 'And I feel the more, Mr. Everett . . . because it was one which my dear father used to wear.'[17] 'Long surtouts were fashionable in the 1780s . . . the neck had from one to two to three broad falling collars known as capes.'[18]

It is not impossible that this is by Sarah (Sally) Wesley junior who, as previously noted, had artistic abilities.

prot. <u>Trewint Cottage, Altarnum, Cornwall, PL15 7TG</u>
Telford gives this as belonging to Dr. [Edward] Riggall. M.R.C.S. (d.1900), who left his collection to his daughter, Mrs E. F. Dodsworth (d. *c.*1945–6). She bequeathed the 'autograph letters (amongst other things)' to Wesley's House in London. The letters at least 'formerly belonged to the Revd. John Gaulter, President of the W.M. Conference, & were purchased by [Riggall] after the death of his surviving Daughter, Miss Gaulter.'[19]

Prints

Johann FABER (1684–1736)   1743

notes. Faber's mezzotint of J. M. Williams's portrait of John Wesley was published in 1743.[20] Some copies are known to exist which are erroneously titled 'Charles Wesley A.M.'.

exmpls. JRRILM.

Patrick MAQUIRE (fl. 1785–1820)   1781

notes. inscr. 'P Maquire, Sc[ulpit]' 8.0 × 6.5 cm. Frontispiece to the *Arminian Magazine*, vol 4 (April 1781), some titled 'Rev^d. Charles Westley'. Stipple; H/S facing L, clergy wig, gown, cassock and bands. Maquire was a Dublin engraver, 'most of his plates . . . are small portraits for the book trade.'[21]

Jonathan SPILSBURY (1737–1812)   1786

inscr. 'J. Spilsbury, delin. ad vivam et sculpit

Charles Wesley A.M.
Presbyter of the Church of England and late Student of Christ Church
LONDON
Published 20th March 1786 by John Atlay, New Chapel, City Road'

notes. Stipple engraving, 315 × 225 cm. HL to L, clergy wig, gown and bands. R arm raised as preaching; L hand rests on book on table. Although an engraving, the inscription indicates clearly that this is from life, by an artist linked to Methodism and published by Wesley's Book Steward.[22] There is no known prototype painting or drawing.

exmpls. NPG D.8226; WHS; Epworth Old Rectory

deriv. William RIDLEY (1766–1838)
Stipple, oval 5.3 × 4.0 cm., undated. Ridley was a 'prolific stipple engraver, primarily of small portraits for periodicals' such as the *Evangelical* and

Arminian (later *Methodist*) *Magazines*.[23] His prints in the *Arminian Magazine*, chiefly in the 1790s, are particularly expressive.

J. FITTLER (1758–1835)   1793

notes.   Bust-length in oval 9.7 × 8.2 cm (overall 12.1 × 10.5 cm.), line engraving. 'Engraved by J. Fittler'. Evidently copied from Spilsbury's print, including the title wording. 'Published as the Act directs, April, 1793, by Dr Whitehead, and engraved for his Life of Mr Wesley.'

Fittler was chiefly a line engraver of scenes; he also engraved William Hamilton's portrait of John Wesley and may have been linked to the Methodists.[24]

W. T. FRY (1789–1843)

Stipple, 17.8 × 10.6 cm. 'Aged 76', suggesting that Spilsbury's delineation was taken *c*.1784. 'London, Published by Mr. Kershaw, 145 City Road.' Kershaw was (Wesleyan) Book Steward 1823–7. William Thomas Fry worked mainly in stipple and exhibited with the Society of British Artists 1829–35. He was one of the first engravers to experiment with steel plates.[25]

J. SHURY

Line/steel, 4.9 × 4.4 cm. closely related to that by Fry, also inscr. 'Aged 76'. H/S only in patterned frame. 'London, Published by Mr. Kershaw, 145 City Road.'

Posthumous Portraits

William GUSH (1813–88)   *c*.1850/1

notes.   H/L, 130 × 106 cm. approx, o/c; behind preaching desk, R hand raised as preaching, L hand rests on open Bible.

Gush showed an early talent for drawing and age eleven became a 'copyist' at the National Gallery. By age twenty he was exhibiting and his work was first hung at the Royal Academy. In 1834 came the first engraving of one of his portraits (Rev. Richard Treffry) for the *Wesleyan Methodist Magazine*: between 1837 and 1861 (like John Jackson RA before him) he provided the great majority of the frontispiece illustrations for the *WM Magazine*. His portrait practice extended well beyond engravings for denominational magazines, and he exhibited regularly at the Royal Academy until 1874.[26]

prot. Kingswood School, Bath. *c.*1851 as painted as a companion to John Russell's portrait of John Wesley for the school's new buildings at Bath in 1851.[27]

print Steel engrv. J. Cochran, 36 × 27 cm. (image 23 x 18 cm.), publ. Nov. 1852 by J. Mason (Wesleyan Book Steward), 14 City Road and 66 Paternoster Row (London). Erroneously captioned as CW born '. . .1708.'

copy Richard DOUGLAS
Acrylic on board, 24 × 30 in., no. 3, *c.*2007, Asbury Theological Seminary, Wilmore, KY 40390

Frederick J. JOBSON (1812–81)   1771

notes. H/L, facing L., 9.5 × 6 in. Clerical wig, gown, preaching bands, heavily dependent on J. Spilsbury's mezzotint (see below), reversed. Illustration in Telford.[28]

Jobson served an apprenticeship with the Gothic revival architect Edward Willson of Lincoln before entering the Wesleyan ministry. Jobson's *Chapel and School Architecture* (1850) was a significant Gothic influence on Methodist buildings. Jobson had a distinguished career as a Wesleyan minister, particularly as Book Steward 1864–79, where he widened the range of publications, and was President of the Conference 1869. Several other small portraits by him are known, jointly with the artist James Smetham (1821–89), who was also apprenticed to Willson.[29]

prot. Given as in the Wesleyan Conference Office, City Road, London, as of 1921.[30] Wesley Swift cited it as in the Book Room (then at Epworth House, City Road) in 1957.[31] Location not now known.

Portraits of Charles Wesley (1707–88)

J. W. L. FORSTER (1850–1938)   *c.*1900

notes. John Wycliffe Lowes Forster, 'a strong supporter of the work of the United Church [of Canada]', visited Britain around 1900 and painted portraits of John and Charles Wesley and their mother, Susanna, for Victoria College, Toronto.[32] Those of John and Charles, in preaching pose, represent heroic perceptions of both.

Prot. <u>Victoria University, Toronto</u> o/c
Oil on canvas, 84 × 54 in. Not now known.

Frank O. SALISBURY (1874–1962)   1957

notes. o/c, 110 × 86 cm., signed. Depicts CW as preaching, heavily dependent on the portrait by Gush. Labelled as 'Quarter millennial memorial portrait', hence the dating of 1957.

prot. World Methodist Museum collection, Bridwell Library, Southern Methodist University, Dallas, TX, U.S.A., from 2021. Formerly at World Methodist Museum, Lake Junaluska, NC, U.S.A., for which it was painted.

Scene Paintings

Robert Ronald McIAN (*c.*1803–1856)   n/d
The Revd. Charles Wesley, Preaching to the North American Indians, 1745

notes. o/c, 44 × 56 in. Actor turned painter, McIan is generally known for romanticised scene-paintings of Scottish history. 'From 1835 to 1856 McIan was a frequent exhibitor at the Royal Academy and elsewhere.'[33] It is not known when or why he depicted this scene; the original canvas was sold through Sothebys 1981, current location unknown.[34] The impossibility of the date (Charles Wesley was only in America for a few months in 1736) and the similarity of the figure to images of John Wesley (but hardly Charles) suggests that this was poorly researched.

engr. F. Bromley 1862 (25 × 32 in.). Steel engraving priced 10/–.

Marshall CLAXTON R.A. (1813–81)   *c.*1858
John Wesley with his Friends at Oxford

notes. The 'Holy Club' was a more informal organisation than Claxton's picture suggests, although he reputedly used the 'actual room', and modelled the figures on contemporary likenesses. A key is known to the individuals featured; Charles Wesley is seated at the table, with his arms raised and hands together.[35] A letter of G. Stevenson (18 October 1851) states that when Claxton left for Australia in 1850 he left behind a painting *The Institution of Methodism* half completed, to be finished by Geller. This may be the picture.[36]

The eponymous son of a Wesleyan minister, Claxton entered the Royal Academy Schools in 1831, possibly having had tuition from the Wesleyan portraitist John Jackson RA (1778–1831). He went to live in Australia in 1850, but was unsuccessful in establishing himself so left in 1854, spending two productive years in India en route. The hugely wealthy Baroness Burdett-Coutts became his sponsor, but his career as an artist was not greatly successful.

prot. Salford Museum and Art Gallery, Manchester (1880–1) o/c, 136.5 × 173.5 cm. 'Presented by Thomas Agnew Esq., 1880'; this work does not appear in the Agnew records.[37]

engr. Bellin 1862 (25 × 32 in.) priced 10/–.

Ralph JOHNSON (1896–1980)   *c.*1949
Charles Wesley Preaching at the Cross, Tanfield, 1742.

notes. Ralph Johnson was a Landscape painter, in oil and watercolour. He was born in Annfield Plain near to Consett. A builder by trade, Johnson chose to paint in his spare time using both oil and watercolour. In 1930 Johnson started to disuse oil and increasingly concentrated on using watercolour alone. Johnson's works were exhibited for many years at the Laing Art Gallery in Newcastle and regularly showed in the Districts Art Society in Durham.[38]

This scene may have been painted specifically for the Durham Big Day, 15 June 1949.[39] The current location of the painting is unknown; the only image known is in the 1949 Big Day brochure.

Richard Gilmore DOUGLAS (b. *c*.1937)   *c*.1999
John Wesley marrying Charles Wesley and Sarah Gwynne

notes.   John Wesley conducted the marriage between Charles Wesley and Sarah Gwynne on 8 April 1749, in Llanlleonfel Church, near Garth.

prot.   John Wesley's Chapel (The 'New Room'), The Horsefair, Bristol NR2011.40, [in gilt and wood frame]. Acrylic on board, 1999, 39.5 × 29.4 cm.

Richard Gilmore DOUGLAS (b. *c*.1937)
Charles Wesley writing

notes.   Acrylic on board, 21 × 17 in., no. 29, n/d, Asbury Theological Seminary, Wilmore, KY 40390. Imagined scene: Charles Wesley seated in armchair with quill; papers on desk by window. Left hand rests on a pet dog.

Statuary

Frederick Brook HITCH (1857–1957)   1938

notes.   Hitch, son of the sculptor Nathaniel Hitch, was a sculptor chiefly of public memorials such as this. The likeness of Charles Wesley is possibly derived chiefly from the portrait print by Jonathan Spilsbury.

prot.   John Wesley's Chapel ('The New Room', Bristol)
Bronze and Horton stone, 200 × 60 × 60 cm (plinth h – 115 cm).[40]

Hobbes VINCENT

notes.   Cast bronze by Schaefer Art Bronze Casting [Arlington, TX]

prot.   Asbury Theological Seminary, Wilmore, Kentucky, KY 40390.

Notes

1. Wesley F. Swift, 'Portraits and Biographies of Charles Wesley, in *Proceedings of the Wesley Historical Society* [henceforth *PWHS*], vol. 31 (1957–8), 86–93, offers an overview, although now outdated. John Telford, *Sayings and Portraits of Charles Wesley* (London, 1927) is of some use although as much devotional as historical.
2. Peter Forsaith, 'Pictorial precocity: John Russell's portraits of Charles and Samuel Wesley' in Nicholas Temperley and Stephen Banfield (eds), *Music and the Wesleys* (Urbana IL, 2010), pp. 150–63, also in *British Art Journal*, vol. X, no. 3 (Winter/Spring 2009–10), 98–103.
3. Richard Chew, *James Everett: a biography* (London, 1875), p. 178.
4. Thomas Jackson, *Recollections of my own Life and Times* (London, 1873), pp. 227–32.
5. See Peter S. Forsaith, *Image, Identity and John Wesley; a study in portraiture* (Abingdon, 2018), p. 96.
6. Richard P. Heitzenrater, 'A Tale of Two Brothers', in *Christian History*, vol. XX, no. 1 (January 2001), 2.
7. Charles H. Kelly, 'The Wesleyan Methodist Book-Room, Pictures in the Book Steward's Room, II', in *Wesleyan Methodist Magazine*, vol. 130 (1907), 735. Kelly was Book Steward 1889–1907, and stated that 'several of the pictures' had come there during his time, though without being specific. [p. 517].
8. In Royal Academy of Music, London [acc. 2003.1061], and see Forsaith, 'Pictorial precocity'.
9. See Peter Forsaith, 'Images of Samuel Wesley', in W. Gibson, *Samuel Wesley and the Crisis of Tory Piety, 1685–1720* (Oxford, 2021), pp. 215–16.
10. Eighteenth-century artists did not habitually sign their work.
11. See Forsaith, *Image, Identity and John Wesley*, p. 165.
12. See George J Stevenson, *Memorials of the Wesley Family* (London, 1876), pp. 476–7; also Forsaith, *Image, Identity and John Wesley*, pp. 59–60, 180–1.
13. John Russell, *Elements of Painting with Crayons* (London, 1772, revised and enlarged 1777).
14. www.npg.org.uk (accessed January 2024).
15. See Kenneth G. C. Newport and Gareth Lloyd (eds), *The Letters of Charles Wesley*, vol. II (Oxford, 2021), pp. 309, 315 etc.
16. Charles Wesley retained the house after they removed to London around 1771.
17. Chew, *James Everett*, p. 179.
18. C. Willett Cunnington and Phillis Cunnington, *Handbook of English Costume in the Eighteenth Century* (London, 1957, revised 1972), p. 222.
19. Telford, *Sayings and Portraits of Charles Wesley*, pp. 154–5, Frank Baker, 'The Dodsworth Bequest' in *PWHS*, vol. 25 (1946), 113–16. John Gaulter (*c.*1765–1839) was President of the Wesleyan Conference 1817.
20. See Forsaith, *Image, identity and John Wesley*, p. 163.
21. David Alexander, *Biographical Dictionary of British and Irish Engravers, 1714–1820* (New Haven CT, 2021), p. 582.
22. Jonathan Spilsbury (1737–1812), see Ruth Young, *Father and Daughter, Jonathan and Maria Spilsbury 1737–1812; 1777–1820* (London, 1952); Charlotte Yeldham, 'A regency artist in Ireland: Maria Spilsbury Taylor (1776–1820)', in *Irish Architectural and Decorative Studies*, vol. viii (2005), 187–219; Alexander, *Biographical Dictionary*, pp. 858–60.
23. Alexander, *Biographical Dictionary*, p. 749.
24. Forsaith, *Image, Identity and John Wesley*, p. 167.
25. www.npg.org.uk (accessed January 2024).

Portraits of Charles Wesley (1707–88)

26 Dee Helmore, *William Gush—Artist, a biography of the 19th century portrait painter*, unpublished study (by a descendant), 2007.

27 'A portrait of John Wesley was brought from the old school. To match this, a portrait of Charles Wesley by Mr. W. Gush was presented by the artist.' A. H. L. Hastling, W. Addington Willis and W. P. Workman, *The history of Kingswood School. . .* (London, 1898), p. 208.

28 Telford, *Sayings and Portraits of Charles Wesley*, pp. 142–3.

29 See 'Jobson, Frederick James, DD' in *Dictionary of Methodism in Britain and Ireland*, [henceforth *DMBI*], https://dmbi.online (accessed January 2024), also in *Oxford Dictionary of National Biography* [henceforth *ODNB*], https://www.oxforddnb.com (accessed January 2024), and B. Gregory, *The life of F. J. Jobson* (London, 1884).

30 [J. Alfred Sharp], *A catalogue of manuscripts and relics, . . . belonging to the Wesleyan Methodist Conference and preserved at the Office of the Conference, City Road, London . . .* (London, 1921), p. 46.

31 Swift, 'Portraits and Biographies of Charles Wesley' in *PWHS*, vol. 31 (1957), 86–93.

32 *Methodist Recorder*, vol X.LII, no. 2300, Winter Number (Christmas 1901), 19–24; http://national.gallery.ca (accessed January 2014).

33 See 'McIan [*née* Whitaker], Frances Matilda [Fanny]' (*c.*1814–97), *ODNB* (accessed November 2023).

34 Sothebys, 28 May 1981, Lot 68.

35 Belden, George *Whitefield—the Awakener*, 2nd edition (London, 1953), facing p. 22. See V. H. H. Green, *The Young Mr Wesley* (London, 1951); Richard P. Heitzenrater, *Mirror and Memory* (Nashville TN, 1989).

36 *PWHS*, vol. 2 (1899), 28–9.

37 Thos. Agnew and Sons Ltd. Archive, National Gallery, London, [NGA27].

38 http://boldonauctions.blogspot.com [auction catalogue 11 April 2018] (accessed November 2023).

39 See 'Durham Methodist Big Meeting' in *DMBI*. 'This was an annual event from 1947 to 1997 on a June Saturday, modelled on the long-established Durham Miners' Gala.'

40 www.artuk.org (accessed November 2023).

'FROM ALL THE *ARTS OF HELL* SECURE': CHARLES WESLEY'S RELATIONSHIP TO JOHN HENDERSON (1757–88)

Jonathan Barry

This essay considers the relationship between John Henderson (1757–88) and the Wesley family, notably Charles Wesley, with particular reference to Henderson's interests in the occult and Wesleyan reactions to this, including the ambivalent response of Adam Clarke. It explores the various intellectual circles around Bristol in which Henderson was situated, and how they related to his close relationship with Charles and his daughter Sally, throwing light on the Wesley family's ecumenical connections in the region. Henderson's universalist theology and exploration of the spirit world attracted a range of responses, from admiration to derision, but to Charles they represented a dangerous set of dealings with 'the arts of hell' from which he hoped to rescue Henderson.

Keywords: Charles Wesley, John Henderson, Methodism, the occult, Bristol

In April 1787, Charles Wesley composed seven hymns in response to the serious illness of John Henderson (1757–88) from which he was not expected to recover. In her notes on these hymns, Charles's daughter Sally recalled that Charles loved John Henderson 'as a son'. Yet few readers of this journal will have heard of Henderson, who, in the words of John Wesley, 'with as great talents as most men in England, had lived two-and-thirty years, and done just nothing'.[1] But in his lifetime, and for some decades after, Henderson achieved substantial fame as an 'extraordinary genius', a largely self-taught child prodigy, polymath and brilliant conversationalist, admired by most of the leading intellectuals of the 1780s. While alive his eccentric lifestyle attracted rival accounts in the

https://doi.org/10.16922/jrhlc.10.2.7

Gentleman's Magazine, and his death prompted yet more, generating a series of biographical essays, which were recycled well into the nineteenth century. Through his protégé, Joseph Cottle, he intrigued the early Romantics: Robert Southey urged Cottle to write his biography, a work which Coleridge also contemplated. There were indeed many parallels between the lives of Coleridge and Henderson, not least the destructive impact of opium in preventing both from completing numerous projects, to their friends' despair.[2] Most notably, Henderson had a deep interest in the 'occult sciences', a fact which, together with his addictions and lack of productivity, made his legacy a deeply ambivalent one, even to those who wished to memorialise his genius.

Until recently, the last biographical account of Henderson was the chapter by Douglas Macleane in his history of Pembroke College, Oxford, which Henderson entered as a twenty-three-year old in 1781, sponsored by former alumnus Josiah Tucker (Dean of Gloucester and Rector of St Stephen's, Bristol), occupying the former room of Dr Johnson, who met him there several times with his friend (and another Bristol patron of Henderson) Hannah More. Macleane's chapter recycles all the earlier stories of Henderson's brilliance and eccentricity, encapsulating the image of a certain type of Oxford intellectual, such as his habit of talking and reading late into the night, then not rising until noon (even when Edmund Burke and Sir Joshua Reynolds knocked on his door!), eccentric dress and hairstyle, odd diet and hygiene practices (cold showers immediately before sleep). Henderson's association with the College (where his portrait, donated by Cottle, still hangs) formed an integral part of his public persona – accounts identify him as 'John Henderson B.A. of Pembroke College, Oxford'.[3]

Recently, Henderson has been rediscovered in another context, that of Bristol and its surrounds, whose literary and intellectual circles nurtured early Romanticism. Prior to attending Pembroke, Henderson taught for a decade in his father's boarding school at Hanham near Bristol and, even before completing his degree in February 1786, Henderson alternated between Oxford and Hanham, spending long periods in the house which his father had (since 1780) converted into a lunatic asylum, recognised for its caring treatment. Henderson was well-known to many of Bristol's intellectuals, including two close friends of Hannah More and Dean Tucker; namely the Rev. Sir James Stonehouse (physician and clergyman) and James Newton, the Baptist pastor and classical tutor at the Bristol Baptist College, who lived with the Cottles. More and Tucker sought to

'From all the *arts of hell* secure'

direct Henderson towards a professional career worthy of his talents, despairing at his refusal either to settle to a major scholarly project or take up a clerical, legal or medical vocation. Friends of theirs offered him opportunities: Burke an entrée to a legal career and William Wilberforce a clerical living. They debated the best means to get this 'voluptuary in learning' to knuckle down to a productive life, speculating whether Dr Johnson might be able to talk sense into him. By the time of his death they seem to have given up on him, although Hannah More (after remonstrating with him by letter in 1787 over his addiction, and urging him to visit her) clearly retained a strong affection for his memory. His portrait, bequeathed by John's father to Hannah's sister Patty, hung in Hannah's sitting room in the 1820s, before being given by her to Cottle, and hence to Pembroke College. There may even have been an (unfulfilled) romantic attachment between Patty (who remained single, like Hannah) and Henderson. Yet Henderson is hardly mentioned in the recent outpouring of scholarly work on Hannah More.[4]

Instead, he has attracted interest through his posthumous impact on Southey, Coleridge and their circle in 1790s Bristol, as mediated by Cottle and his 'Monody' on Henderson, first published, together with a sketch of Henderson's character, in Cottle's *Poems* (Bristol, 1795). Of the poets around Cottle, only William Gilbert, author of *The Hurricane* (Bristol, 1797), knew Henderson personally, having been treated in his father's asylum in 1788, where John encouraged Gilbert's astrological speculations on the number 666. Paul Cheshire, Gilbert's biographer, has provided the best recent account of Henderson, finally moving beyond the 'Oxford eccentric' stereotype to capture the range of his career, in particular his impact on the young Bristolian Robert Southey, another omnivorous reader and polymath, anxious both about his own career and the dangerous intellectual paths he and his friends were following. These themes are also explored in Brian Goldberg's study of the 'professional identity' of the Lake Poets, examining Coleridge and Southey's poetic responses to Cottle's 'Monody', in which Henderson represents an attractive model of intellectual daring and depth, spurning worldly advance, yet also a warning figure. Goldberg contrasts their response with that of Cottle himself, who had tamed Henderson (he argues) by highlighting Henderson's religious character, justifying his lack of achievement in this world by arguing that he would fulfil his pedagogic destiny in the next world. Cheshire and Goldberg build on Tim Whelan's recovery of the vibrant intellectual circles of the Bristol Baptists from which Cottle had emerged, notably James Newton and Caleb Evans and their pupils Robert Hall and Joseph Hughes. These men, politically liberal though theologically quite conservative (at least anti-Unitarian), must, like Stonehouse, More and Tucker, have provided an important intellectual setting for Henderson, as stimulating perhaps as that offered in Oxford.[5]

However, this welcome new perspective on Henderson has tended to obscure the other circle in which he must be understood, that of Wesleyan Methodism, and particularly his close relationship to Charles Wesley, which is the theme of this essay. John's father Richard, originally from Ireland (where John was born, near Limerick, in 1757) came over to England in 1762 as a Wesleyan itinerant preacher, serving in Bristol and other parts of southern England until 1771, when he opened his school at Hanham. He (or perhaps his wife Charlotte, apparently from a Welsh gentry family like Sarah Wesley, Charles's wife) clearly tired of itinerancy, but Richard was, like his son, very keen on books and philosophy. In 1801, Methodist biographer Charles Atmore considered that Richard had wasted his evangelical talents because of his over-intellectual tendencies, judging that his family tragedies had perhaps been divine punishment for this.[6] Yet, Richard remained close to both John and Charles Wesley. John Wesley's diary (supplementing his published *Journals*) show twice-yearly visits to Richard at Hanham during his regular stays in Bristol, and he publicly praised Richard's piety, humanity and skill in his care for the insane (including several people from Methodist backgrounds, such as William Gilbert), although he noted that despite being 'the best physician for lunatics in England', Richard 'could not save the life of his only son! Who was probably taken to bring his father to God!' Despite this damning final verdict on John's wasted life, John Wesley was full of compassion for his father's grief.[7]

The Hendersons were even closer to Charles Wesley and his family (who lived in Bristol from the mid-1750s to 1771 and frequently visited thereafter), especially his daughter Sally (1759–1828). William Wilberforce recalled, for example, that he had met the Wesleys through Hannah More at Richard Henderson's, recalling a tea party in *c.*1786 at More's when Charles 'rose from the teatable' and 'gave me solemnly his blessing'. Sally's statement that Charles loved Henderson 'as a son', is reflected in the seven hymns in which Charles explored John's failure to fulfil what the Wesleys clearly saw as his proper vocation, namely as a preacher or writer leading people to God. The hymns express an intense desire that, if spared, John would henceforth dedicate his life to this public good, not to self-indulgent study. Charles Wesley died shortly before John Henderson, but 'Sarah Wesley' (either Sally or her mother) wrote to Richard after John's death: in his reply he refers to a 'manuscript . . . entrusted to his son' that has been passed 'to Miss Stafford according to Sarah's wish', and that Charles had 'often spoke' of his diary being 'revised' by John, but nothing ever came of it. In his will, Richard conditionally bequeathed a golden seal of John's to Sally Wesley, and there was talk of their possible marriage (though Cottle denied that John was any more attached to her than to several other women).[8]

John's early life was indeed shaped by his father's Wesleyan work. He attended Kingswood School (close to Hanham), where by age eight he was apparently teaching the other pupils. Even more extraordinarily, when Trevecca College was opened by the Countess of Huntingdon for the adult education of promising evangelical itinerants, John, aged 12 or 13, became the classics teacher. In 1771 the College was riven by the dispute within evangelical circles between Calvinism and Arminianism, which led John Fletcher of Madeley to withdraw as president, and John left Trevecca at the same time. Whether he was dismissed because the precocious youngster had already taken a theological stand against Calvinism is not clear. Perhaps he was called back to help his father in his new school, or did Richard establish the school partly to give his prodigious son a secure place to live with his family? If so, such security was shattered by his mother's death in 1775: John never recovered from this loss, regularly spending the night lying on his mother's grave at St George's, Kingswood, where he would also be buried. His biographies state that John was deeply troubled during his childhood, as reflected in a poem on the death of a pet goldfinch (published posthumously in 1792) which, even allowing for poetic licence, seems exceptionally melancholic. His father was so devastated at John's death that he had his son's body disinterred a few days after his burial in case he was alive, and continued grieving until his own death in 1792.[9]

As a teenager, John underwent a period of religious seeking. He stated later that he owed his escape from 'some prejudices of education' to 'the candour of my father who, though he inculcated his own principles on me, left me to my own judgment.' His biographers testify to his comprehensive knowledge of all religious systems, while presenting a (rather comfortable) image of him as someone sympathetic to all religious opinions but committed to no particular denomination, though ultimately orthodox. His Anglican patrons, in particular, were keen to stress that his refusal to take holy orders was not out of any religious scruples, while his Wesleyan and Baptist admirers were also convinced that he had firmly rejected not only atheism and infidelity but also the more insidious (to their eyes) Socinianism and Unitarianism. Yet in 1774 we find the young Henderson corresponding with the Socinian Joseph Priestley, then living at Calne in Wiltshire, who answered his letters and both lent and gave him books: at that date he was still in doubt about 'the Trinity and the Mediation of Christ', though he believed 'that the prophecies in our Bible were given by God; that the Gospels are true; that whatever we believe should accord with the speeches of Christ therein recorded' and that the doctrine of original sin was absurd. In 1775 he wrote to John Wesley (in a letter published, probably edited, by Wesley in the *Arminian Magazine* for 1787) assuring him that, despite his many remaining uncertainties, he was now secure in his faith in the divinity and atoning role of Jesus.[10] His most distinctive doctrine was universalism, a position which attracted much support at this period, not least from Sir George Stonehouse (cousin of Sir James) who lived in nearby north Somerset. By 1774 he considered 'the pains of hell are purgatory' and John's two surviving published statements on religion both express this universalism, with its belief that a loving God must ultimately intend the redemption of all mankind, so that the punishments of hell are purgatorial, not eternal, and that this reflected mankind's origin in God's provision (following the rebellion of the angels), of a choice to fallen angels to take material form as men, foreseeing a path of salvation through the merits of Christ.[11]

The contemporary biographies of this 'genius' portray John as a solitary reader, absorbing all these ideas from books (especially the works of the 'Schoolmen', such as Duns Scotus and Aquinas, as well as the classics and modern philosophers and theologians) and forming his own intellectual systems. Yet this image may underplay his debt to the intellectuals around him. In addition to those already identified, we should note his membership of two local groups. The first was the Burnham Society, founded by Richard Locke of Burnham in Somerset, a curious amalgam of friendly society and debating group (apparently inspired by Trevecca) which attracted an extraordinary range of religious thinkers, including John Fletcher, George Stonehouse, the future Swedenborgian leader Robert Hindmarsh, and John Wesley (who preached there). Locke's publication in 1798 of selected materials (primarily universalist in character) from their proceedings includes a long letter by Henderson.[12] The second was the Bath Philosophical Society (1779–87), started by Henderson's close friend the Quaker Edmund Rack (1735–87), of which Henderson was one of twenty-five members. William Matthews (1747–1816), another Bath Quaker, was also a member, and Henderson contributed a 'postscript' to the 'dissertation on eternal punishment' in the third volume (on the nature of spirits) of Matthews' *Miscellaneous Companions* (Bath, 1786).[13]

Both these groups were self-consciously ecumenical, determined to put philosophical truth-seeking ahead of denominational distinctions, and this no doubt appealed to the 'seeker' in Henderson, but he was far from being a lone seeker. Indeed, he was particularly close to another Quaker 'seeker', John Till Adams (1748–86), described as 'a worthy and ingenious physician, by profession a Quaker, with whom and Mr Henderson an intimacy subsisted closer than is usually to be found between brothers and which continued undiminished till death'. Till Adams came to Bristol in the late 1770s, after apprenticeship as a surgeon-apothecary, but took up the practice of physic (obtaining an Aberdeen MD in 1780): controversially he and his wife Ann (from the Quaker Fry family of Bristol) ran a druggist's shop even after he became a physician, and following his early death she and other family members continued as druggists.[14] Till Adams worked closely with the Baptist physician Abraham Ludlow (d. 1807), a close friend of Charles Wesley's family, who attended John in his 1787 illness, informing his father Richard admiringly that John 'is all mind'.[15] Till Adams was, like John, deeply interested in astrology and alchemy, adopting the Paracelsian tradition in medicine, and both men displayed Paracelsus's disdain for the normal mores of the medical profession, reflected not only in Till Adams's insistence on supplying his own prescriptions, but also in supplying the needs of the poor free of charge. Henderson and Till Adams treated the sick together in Bristol and John continued the practice in Oxford, famously selling his cherished polyglot Bible to raise funds for medicines he prescribed during a fever epidemic, from which he also fell ill. He notoriously tried out numerous dangerous medications (including musk and mercury) on himself (again, a Paracelsian practice), and his opium addiction may have originated in the same way (the firm Till Adams's widow continued later specialised in the opium-based medicine, nepthalene).

Till Adams, like many Quakers, was also influenced by mystic religious traditions such as Behmenism, quietism and then Swedenborgianism.

He shared these interests with his friend Ebenezer Sibly, who lived at Bristol between 1784 and 1787, developing under Till Adams's influence from an astrologer into a Paracelsian medical practitioner before moving to London (and taking an Aberdeen MD in 1792). The final volume of Sibly's *New and Complete Illustration of Astrology* (1784–8) includes an astrological account of Henderson, complete with a chart and image by the Bristol engraver Ames. Although his brother Manoah became a Swedenborgian minister, Ebenezer remained on the fringes, drawing eclectically on traditions such as Behmenism and animal magnetism which led many to Swedenborg, but also on older occult sources. The same is true of Henderson, who was widely read in, and sympathetic to, Behmen, Law and Swedenborg but did not become a disciple of any of them.[16]

Henderson wrote relatively little, preferring conversation, and almost all his manuscripts were destroyed, either accidentally (by a servant) or deliberately by him or an (unnamed) female correspondent after his death (Sally Wesley or Patty More?).[17] Those commenting on his involvement in the occult sciences do so from a hostile, or at least very ambivalent, perspective. One example is Josiah Tucker's 1782 letter to Hannah More reporting on 'our little philosopher' Henderson (who he is surprised to find staying at Hanham with his father and 'Friend Rick [i.e. Edmund Rack] of Bath' rather than keeping term in Oxford). 'I find that I have been truly informed concerning him, that he believes in witches and apparitions, as well as in judicial astrology. And though he bears the raillery very well, and joins in it with a good grace, yet I do not find that any thing that can be said, has any influence to make him change his opinion.' Before considering his own proposal for setting 'this eccentric genius on some work . . . pleasant to himself, as well as useful to the public', Tucker indulges in a flight of fancy:

> Should all other schemes fail, you and your female friends at Oxford have it in your power to make him as rich as a nabob, by giving out that he is the *true original conjuror*, whom Shakspeare [*sic*] consulted on all occasions when he introduced witches; and that he has made so many voyages to the stars since that time, that there is not a Madam *Hotspur* throughout the kingdom, whose fortune he could not tell at the shortest notice. A handsome genteel set of apartments somewhere about St. James's, with a white wand and a long artificial beard, would be all the accoutrements necessary, (with such good

'From all the *arts of hell* secure'

assistance,) to set him up in high life both above stairs and below. Such a hint might be improved upon, and a female genius is particularly happy in the necessary embellishments on such occasions.[18]

Setting aside the gender stereotyping here (of astrology as appealing to fashionable female folly, as well as vulgar female credulity), it is clear that Tucker has an anxiety (expressible only in humour) that Henderson might follow the very career that Sibly (and Gilbert, briefly) adopted.

Charles Wesley's hymns during Henderson's illness reflect the same concern, but whereas Tucker regarded John's beliefs as ridiculous, Wesley considered them spiritually dangerous.[19] Within his overall theme that this illness was a God-sent opportunity for John to redeem his life ('If hitherto, intirely Thine, He has not answer'd thy Design, Or Liv'd for God alone, But stoop'd admiring Crouds to please; Thy Servant, Lord, this moment seize, and seal him all thine own.'), Charles wishes God to 'lead him on From all the *arts of hell* secure, To make his glorious calling sure'. Later, in a hymn written as if spoken by John himself, he admits 'Idle I in the vineyard stood, Or vain philosophy pursued, Eager, athirst to know The mysteries of earth and sky, And skill'd in *curious arts* to pry Into the depths below. But lo! I from this moment turn To Thee.' In another hymn he has John, in asking God to 'Explain the language of thy Rod' (i.e. the meaning of his illness), wondering:

Is it some unacknowledg'd sin That forces mercy to chastise? I fear the secret Cause to know, But cannot from thy sight conceal; Omniscient God the Evil show, The mysteries of Hell reveal. In an angelical disguise, If Satan did my soul deceive Thou canst detect his specious lies And wisdom to thy Servant give: Against the Israelitish race, In vain the fiend his pow'r exerts Thy Spirit shall the Demon ['Sorcerer' is written above this in the manuscript as a possible alternative] chase, And baffle all his curious arts.

He continues 'After my Lord resolv'd to go, And do whate'er thy laws require, I trample on th'infernal Foe, And cast *his* books into the fire: Thy Book my Rule and Study still.' Sally Wesley added a note below this particular hymn:

Before John Henderson died (on whom and for whom these Lines were written by the Revd Charles Wesley) He earnestly entreated that all his Books on Magic might be burnt. He expressed the utmost self-abasement, and whole dependence on the blessed Redeemer, without whom (he said) Heaven would be no Heaven to him. He departed this Life in 1788 a few months after the Revd Charles Wesley – by whom He was beloved as a Son.[20]

In this Wesleyan reading, John's pursuit of 'the curious arts' was a diabolic temptation from which he required redemption. This view found crude re-statement in the biography published in the *Arminian Magazine* in 1793:

He descended into the depths of *Jacob Behmen's* wild philosophical divinity, and became an admirer of the profound nonsense that abounds in the dark regions of mysticism. He not only expended much precious time in the study of *Lavater's* Physiognomy, but, what was far more reprehensible, he attained to a considerable knowledge of the occult sciences of Magic and Astrology! His library was well stored with the magical and astrological books of the last century! He has, at times, ventured to declare the possibility of holding a correspondence with separate spirits, upon the strength of his own experience![21]

Yet it is from a leading Wesleyan of the next generation, Adam Clarke, that we have an account of Henderson's involvement in magic, written not in condemnation but in the context of Clarke's own occult interests. Like Richard Henderson, Clarke was from Ireland, attending Kingswood School briefly in 1782 before starting on his Methodist itinerancy, which led to a career of theological and linguistic scholarship that made him the most respected Wesleyan scholar of the early nineteenth century. Indeed, Clarke fulfilled the promise that Henderson had only shown: armed with polyglot Bible and a largely self-taught grasp of numerous languages and bodies of knowledge, he combined impeccable evangelical achievement with an extensive learned output across many fields. Yet Clarke's autobiographical notes, published posthumously, reveal his fascination when young with books of enchantment and magic, including his long search for a copy of the *Occult Philosophy* of Cornelius Agrippa. While rejoicing that providence protected him from trying to carry out its actual spells, Clarke justified his childhood enthusiasm for enchantments and spirits as a healthy alternative to the much greater dangers of 'modern Sadducism', laying the groundwork for his exploration of the higher spiritual truths of the Scriptures.[22] His autobiography does not refer explicitly to the Hendersons (though the day he left Kingswood, he went to Hanham en route to Bath), but we learn of their links through the account in *Adam Clarke Portrayed* (1843) by James Everett. Many decades later, when the Rev. John Lomas asked him his 'serious opinion of Magic', Clarke replied: 'There is scarcely an error, Sir, but what has something of truth for its origin or foundation and scarcely a truth that has not been abused. Magic has been abused.' When another person in the conversation described the belief that spirits can be raised as 'too ridiculous to be believed', Clarke responded by telling them about a visit he had made:

> to the father of the celebrated John Henderson, who kept a seminary near Bristol. He never looked up after the death of John, and never could advert to it without the most acute pain. He had everything belonging to him, locked up. I was permitted one day to see John's library, which was no common privilege. I saw books there, on Magic &c, which I had never seen before; they were extremely rare; I could almost have stolen them, had I known how to come at them. Dr Priestley once asked John very pointedly, 'Did you ever see a spirit? he replied, – 'I cannot say, I never did.' There the subject rested between them. John used to take the lantern and candle, go out into the fields at night, fix his rods, form his circles, &c.

As Everett notes, Clarke used this anecdote about John to divert the subject from himself, but his own deep fascination by (if not belief in) magic was 'confirmed by the books he purchased on several of the hidden arts', demonstrated by the printed catalogue of his library at death, from which Everett cites 'treatises on alchemy, astrology, witchcraft, chiromancy, magic, conversations with spirits &c'. Everett equivocates, wishing not to 'condemn such pursuits in one, who, when Christianized, guarded against the abuses made of them by many others' but unwilling to promote Clarke's example, given that the vast majority of people drawn to such pursuits would not be able to avoid abuses.[23] Assuming Clarke's anecdote to be true (and it must date from 1789–90, when he served in Bristol for a year, frustratingly hardly discussed in his autobiography), then it seems that Henderson's father, or someone else in his circle, believed that John had actually attempted conjuration. It also suggests that neither John nor Richard fulfilled John's promise to Charles Wesley to burn his books of magic. Richard donated his books (presumably including John's) to his co-executor, Robert de Joncourt (the French teacher at Kingswood 1787–9), but their subsequent fate is unknown.

The question of Henderson's involvement in the occult resonated throughout the public discussions of his character and legacy. William Agutter's funeral sermon, despite offering a detailed account of Henderson, largely ignored this subject, simply noting that 'he would not join the indolent cry of Ignorance and Affectation to brand with odium the occult sciences, before he had examined them for himself'.[24] This did not convince Richard Gough, reviewing the sermon for the *Gentleman's Magazine*, who observes drily that 'he was a most orthodox Christian, and carried his credulity to its utmost excess in theology and everything else (for he believed in witchcraft, demonology, judicial astrology and the philosopher's stone) . . . This was the natural consequence of his being a teacher in the college of Treveka'.[25] This drew a response from Walter Churchey, the Wesleyan lawyer brought up near Trevecca, claiming that Henderson 'kept his own real sentiments upon metaphysical subjects to an excess in reserve; so that it may be difficult for us to prove, that he was credulous to excess in witchcraft, demonology, judicial astrology, and that pretty fable the philosopher's stone; not to add, as you say, in theology, and everything else.' However, 'I can bring one instance of his caution on the subject of demonology myself. I applied to him, to know his thoughts on a late affair in Bristol, in which Mr Easterbrook was concerned, whose religious, moral and rational character, there, is too well established to be shaken by pointless ridicule from that or any other quarter. Mr H. so far from showing his credulity, gave me no reply.'[26] Churchey then carefully distances himself from vulgar or female credulity (aunts' and grandmothers' tales of 'Hobgoblins, Jack-o'-lanterns, Will-o'-wisps, and Jack-o'-Kent'), arguing that Henderson would not risk his reputation 'to give credit to any tale, unsupported by stubborn facts, exceedingly well-attested'.

> But supposing he had believed in the present possibility of witchcraft and demonology, or even in the appearance of disembodied spirits, no less a precedent than Mr Addison seemed to go *very near* such credulity, if you must attach that name to such sort of faith . . . If Mr H. was or was not fond of, or did or did not understand, any thing of judicial astrology, it matters not; it may be a science of

> curiosity for inquisitive minds; and he had as much right to study it, as others have to blame him for so doing . . . I blame no man for trying all things, if he holds fast that which is best, viz. the love of God and man.

Churchey adds 'I have reason, personally, to know' that Gough was mistaken to trace any credulity to his time at Trevecca. While 'most ably instructing the students there in the learned languages', Henderson 'was often arguing against the inconsistencies of their idol doctrine, Calvinism' and he was dismissed 'because he was not an orthodox Christian and did not carry his credulity to its utmost excess in theology, and in everything else'.[27]

I have explored more fully in another essay Henderson's position on the occult, and the contemporary responses it engendered.[28] A number of common themes emerge in both the condemnations and the defences of his behaviour, and particularly in the efforts to strike a balance between the two. These include the distinction between scholarly exploration of the occult tradition, appropriate both to a genius and to a dedicated scholar, on the one hand, and the possible misuse of this knowledge as disseminated to those incapable of avoiding its abuse. What could be discussed safely in male circles of philosophical enlightenment (many of them deeply religious) would be dangerous if abused. This concern overlapped with a second requirement, namely that Henderson should put his learning to the public good, either through scholarly output or through a vocation as a cleric/preacher (or preferably both, as Clarke managed), subordinating a selfish pursuit of knowledge for its own sake to higher ends. This in turn was associated with a clear distinction between that aspect of esoteric knowledge which could be turned to pastoral profit, namely its testimony regarding the nature of God's spiritual creation and purposes, and that aspect which involved the illicit attempt to pry into, even control, the spirits themselves, potentially for self-advancement. The 'conjuror', who attempted the conjuration of spirits using ritual methods, was the unacceptable face: but the man of God who was open to the voluntary communication of knowledge and guidance from the spiritual world, and was willing to testify to the reality of this 'world of spirits' against the claims of infidelity and materialism, was a different matter.

Of course, the exact nature and import of this spiritual communication, and its significance compared to other sources of knowledge, was highly debated both between and within different religious traditions. It was generally more valued by the pietistic and evangelical traditions than by those content with the established pastoral provision of the Church, and perhaps least valued by the liberal Unitarian tradition. But these distinctions were not hard and fast ones, and could be overridden by personal interests and ties, by the pressure of circumstances (especially during the millenarian anxieties and hopes of the period 1776–1815), and by contradictions within the esoteric tradition itself. At the heart of these lay anxiety about whether the testimony of the spirit world could indeed be reliably derived, given the ever-present threat posed by the 'father of lies', the Devil. Willingness to take this risk depended on a difficult balancing act reflecting, ultimately, one's sense of how God's providence operated. Pessimists, including Charles Wesley, feared God's justice towards sinning man would permit him to allow the Devil to mislead even the best-intentioned, while optimists (like the universalist Henderson) hoped that God's mercy would ensure that their good intentions would keep them safe. Yet both traditions knew they were treading a narrow path. The lives of men like Henderson were fascinating precisely because they offered an intriguing example of someone treading this path, whose early death left the meaning of his life profoundly open-ended.

Notes

[1] H. Moore, *Life of the Rev. John Wesley*, vol. 2 (London, 1825), pp. 360–1. Henderson does not appear, for example, in G. M. Best, *Charles Wesley* (Peterborough, 2006) or K. G. C. Newport and T. A. Campbell (eds), *Charles Wesley: Life, literature and legacy* (Peterborough, 2007), though he is discussed (but without reference to his connection to Charles and Sally Wesley) in G. M. Best, *The Cradle of Methodism* (Bristol, 2017), pp. 404–6. Substantial portions of this essay, written in 2018, have also appeared in my essay, 'John Henderson (1757–1788) and Changing Attitudes to the Occult in Enlightenment England', in J. Hedesan and T. Rudboeg (eds) *The Old in the New: Historical Transformations of Western Esotericism from the Middle Ages to the Present* (Cham, 2021), pp. 155–83.

[2] B. Cottle, *Joseph Cottle and the Romantics* (Bristol, 2008), pp. 4–13, 73, 153–5, 299–300; K. Curry (ed.), *New Letters of Robert Southey* (New York and London, 1965), pp. 126–7, 367; B. Goldberg, *The Lake Poets and Professional Identity* (Cambridge, 2007), pp. 34–45, 149; N. Roe (ed.), *English Romantic Writers and the West Country* (Basingstoke, 2010); P. Cheshire, 'Genius and Its Abuses: Southey's Wary Fascination with John Henderson', *Wordsworth Circle*, vol. 42, no. 1 (2011), 17–22. I am very grateful to Paul Cheshire for sharing his findings on Henderson with me.

[3] D. Macleane, *A History of Pembroke College Oxford* (Oxford Historical Society, XXXIII, 1897), pp. 397–406; this approach is reflected also in his *Dictionary of National Biography*

and revised *Oxford Dictionary of National Biography* entries: see J. Sambrook, 'Henderson, John (1757–1788), student and eccentric', https://www.oxforddnb.com (accessed 27 January 2024).

4 J. Cottle, *Poems* (Bristol, 1795), pp. 108–22; Cottle, *Poems*, 2nd edition (Bristol, 1796), pp. 99–122; Cottle, *Malvern Hills*, 2 vols. (London, 1829), vol. 1, pp. 349–71 and vol. 2, pp. 339–46; Cottle, *Reminiscences of Samuel Taylor Coleridge and Robert Southey* (London, 1847), pp. 2, 42–3, 53–6, 340–1, 488–99; S. T. Coleridge, *Poems*, 2nd edition (Bristol, 1797), p. 248; J. Watkins, *The Peeper; A Collection of Essays Moral, Biographical and Literary, to which are Added Biographical Memoirs of Mr John Henderson, A.B. and the Rev. Mr Samuel Badcock*, 2nd edition (London, 1798), pp. 298–300; Watkins, 'Memoir of Mrs Hannah More', in *The Works of Hannah More . . . with a Memoir and Notes*, vol. 1 (London, 1834), pp. 9, 22, 61; W. Roberts (ed.), *Memoirs of the Life and Correspondence of Mrs Hannah More*, 3rd edition (London, 1835), vol. 1, pp. 194–6, 216–21, 261–2, 277, and vol. 2, p. 140; J. M. Traherne, 'Letters of Miss Hannah More etc', *Gentleman's Magazine* (August 1840), 132–6; H. J. Foster, 'John Henderson, Dean Tucker and Hannah More', *Proceedings of the Wesley Historical Society* [hereafter *PWHS*], vol. 3, no. 6 (1902), 162–5; Cottle, *Joseph Cottle*, pp. 9, 13, 162, 253. Anne Stott, *Hannah More* (Oxford, 2003) does not mention John Henderson, though More's visits to his father's asylum (where she paid for the care of 'Louisa, the maid of the haystacks') are described on pp. 55–7.

5 See n 2 and W. Gilbert, 'Explanation of the Number 666', *Conjuror's Magazine*, vol. 1, no. 7 (1792), 220–4; T. Whelan, 'Joseph Cottle the Baptist', *Charles Lamb Bulletin*, no. 111 (2000), 96–108; Paul Cheshire's website on William Gilbert at www.williamgilbert.com

6 C. Atmore, *The Methodist Memorial* (London, 1801), pp. 183–5.

7 *Bristol Journal*, 21 September 1771; Bristol Archives, Henderson Family Notes, 39801/F/22; H. J. Foster, 'Richard Henderson and his Private Asylum at Hanham', *PWHS*, vol. 3, no. 6 (1902), pp. 158–61; J. Telford (ed.), *Letters of the Rev. John Wesley AM*, vol. 8 (London, 1931), pp. 87, 107, 230; C. R. Hudleston, 'Richard Henderson of Hanham', *Notes and Queries*, vol. 175 (1938), pp. 409–10; Bicentennial Edition of *The Works of John Wesley*, general editors Frank Baker, Richard P. Heitzenrater, and Randy L. Maddox (Oxford: Clarendon Press, 1975–83, and Nashville: Abingdon Press, 1984–) [henceforth identified as *Works*, followed by volume and page numbers], 23:224, 230–2, 297, 377, 462–3, 479, 500, 535, 572; and 24:108, 123, 156 (quoted), 275.

8 R. and S. Wilberforce, *The Life of William Wilberforce* (London, 1843), p. 123; John Rylands Research Institute and Library, University of Manchester, Methodist Archives and Research Centre (hereafter MMA), Charles Wesley papers, letters from John Henderson to Charles Wesley of 26 February 1787, GB 133 DDPr 1/36; from Richard Henderson to Charles Wesley dated 12 April 1787, in reply to a 'kind and affectionate letter' from Charles during John's illness, GB 133 DDPr 1/37; from Richard Henderson to Sarah Wesley dated 23 July 1788, GB 133 DDPr 1/38; and from Charles Wesley to his wife and children from Bristol dated 2 September 1787?, MMA, DDWes4/71: when they arrive there 'they will be met by John Henderson'; Cottle, *Reminiscences*, pp. 212–13; The National Archives, will of Richard Henderson dated 31 October 1791, proved 5 March 1792, Prob 11/1216/40; Cottle, *Joseph Cottle*, pp. 72–3 (*ibid*, p. 13, claims Sally Wesley was a frequent visitor to the Cottle family house when Joseph was young, but no reference is given). Very little attention has been paid to Sally compared to Charles's two musical sons, the fullest account being in G. Stevenson, *Memorials of the Wesley Family* (London, 1876), pp. 471–89, but even this has little to say about her life in Bristol, though her continuing attachment to the city after 1771 is made clear and she retired there before her death.

9   Watkins, *Peeper*, pp. 294–9; A. C. H. Seymour, *Life and Times of Selina Countess of Huntingdon*, vol. 2 (London, 1844), p. 197; L. Tyerman, *Wesley's Designated Successor* (London, 1882), p. 145; A. Harding, *Countess of Huntingdon's Connexion* (Oxford, 2003), chapter V; 'Lines on the Death of a Favourite Goldfinch by the late Mr J. Henderson, written when he was very young', *European Magazine*, vol. 22 (July–December 1792), 235–6. Best, *Cradle*, p. 404 suggests that in 1771 John returned to teach at Kingswood, but this is based on the mistaken belief that Joseph Cottle was taught by John at Kingswood, whereas he attended Richard Henderson's school (Cottle, *Joseph Cottle*, pp. 4–6).

10 J. Priestley, 'Original Letters from Mr Henderson to Dr Priestley', *Gentleman's Magazine*, vol. 59 (1789), 287; [J. Henderson], 'Letter CCCCXLI. From Mr J. H. to the Rev. J. Wesley. Hannam-Green, Oct. 1, 1775', *The Arminian Magazine*, vol. 10 (1787), 662–3.

11 [R. Locke], *The Pre-existence of Souls and Universal Restitution Considered as Scripture Doctrines* (Taunton, 1798), pp. 15–19; [J. Henderson] 'Postscript to the Dissertation on Eternal Punishment', in W. Matthews (ed.), *The Miscellaneous Companion*, vol. 3 (Bath, 1786) pp. 111–15, reprinted in R. Southey, *Letters Written during a Short Residence in Spain and Portugal* (Bristol, 1797), pp. 529–32.

12 Locke, *Pre-existence*, esp. p. 50 and fn; R. Southey, *Life of Wesley*, vol. 2 (London, 1846), p. 597; H. J. Foster, 'Burnham Society, Somerset', *Notes and Queries*, vol. 9, no 224 (11 April 1908), 291–2; F. M. Ward (ed.), *Supplement to Collinson's History of Somerset by Richard Locke* (Taunton, 1939), pp. 16–19; G. Rowell, 'A Note on the History and Doctrine of the Burnham Society', *PWHS*, vol. 37, no. 1 (1969), 10–16.

13 Matthews, *Miscellaneous Companion*; L. Klein, 'Hierarchy and the Techniques of the Mediator', *Cultural and Social History*, vol. 10 (2013), pp. 489–510. Rack (along with Hannah More) was a friend of Richard Polwhele, the Cornish clergyman and antiquarian, and wrote to him in March 1782 when Polwhele was a student at Oxford to urge him to make Henderson's acquaintance: R. Polwhele, *Traditions and Recollections* (London, 1826), pp. 75, 134–6.

14 Watkins, *Peeper*, pp. 300–1; W. Churchey, 'The Character of Mr Henderson more fully Delineated', *Gentleman's Magazine*, vol. 59 (June 1789), 504; M. Dresser (ed.), *The Diary of Sarah Fox née Champion* (Bristol Record Society, 55, 2003), pp. 65–6.

15 John Rylands Research Institute and Library, MMA, GB 133 DDPr 1/37. For a poem by Charles to 'his much respected friend Dr Ludlow' (Abraham, not 'Edmund' as suggested by the editors) in 1774 see, MMA DDWes/1/56; Ludlow's life to 1799 (he died in 1807) is described in a letter by Jane March to Mary Fletcher c.February 1799 in MMA MAM/FL/5/2/7.

16 E. Sibly, *A New and Complete Illustration* (London, 1784–8), pp. 798–800; J. Barry, *Raising Spirits* (Basingstoke, 2013), pp. 81–7; S. M. Sommers, *The Siblys of London* (Oxford, 2018), pp. 60–7.

17 'F', 'Art. X: *A Sermon Occasioned by the Death of the Celebrated Mr J. Henderson B.A. of Pembroke College*', *Analytical Review*, vol. 3 (1789), 297–309. I cannot establish the identity of 'F', who reviewed regularly.

18 Roberts (ed.), *Memoirs*, vol. 1, p. 217.

19 For the Wesleys and the occult see Henry Rack, *Reasonable Enthusiast* (London, 1989); Rack, 'Charles Wesley and the Supernatural', *Bulletin of the John Rylands University Library of Manchester*, vol. 88 (2006), 59–79; Robert Webster, *Methodism and the Miraculous* (Lexington KY, 2013). For the place of illness and healing in Charles Wesley's hymns see Webster, 'Balsamic Virtue' in Newport and Campbell (eds), *Charles Wesley*, pp. 229–44.

20 John Rylands Research Institute and Library, MMA, MS Henderson, MA 1977/594/1, transcript available online from Duke University, at https://divinity.duke.edu/sites/divinity.duke.edu/files/documents/cswt/44_MS_Henderson.pdf (accessed 24 October 2023).

21 'Anecdotes of John Henderson, B.A.', *The Arminian Magazine*, vol. 16 (1793), 140–4.

22 J. B. B. Clarke (ed.), *An Account of the Religious and Literary Life of Adam Clarke* (New York, 1837), pp. 66–7, 146, 218.

23 J. Everett, *Adam Clarke Portrayed*, vol. 1 (London, 1843), pp. 74–9.

24 W. Agutter, *A Sermon Occasioned by the Death of the Celebrated Mr J. Henderson B.A. of Pembroke College* (Bristol, 1788), p. 5 (though pp. 4–6, 13 and 25 indicate Agutter's belief in higher beings, angels, an invisible world and God communicating without using 'the outward sense').

25 [R. Gough], 'Review of William Agutter's *A Sermon occasioned by the Death of the celebrated Mr. J. Henderson*', *Gentleman's Magazine*, vol. 59 (February 1789), 151–2.

26 This refers to the exorcism of George Lukins by Easterbrook, the vicar of Temple, Bristol, in 1788: see J. Barry, *Witchcraft and Demonology in South-West England* (Basingstoke, 2012), pp. 206–55. John Wesley frequently preached at Temple for Easterbrook when in Bristol: for Charles doing so see MMA DD/Wes/4/44 (7 August 1786).

27 Churchey, 'Character', pp. 503–7. For Churchey see Cottle, *Joseph Cottle*, p. 162 and W. I. Morgan, 'Walter Churchey, 1747–1805', *Brycheiniog*, vol. 16 (1972), 79–102. John Wesley discussed the Hendersons in a letter to his niece Sarah Wesley of 8 September 1788 (Telford, *Letters*, 8:88); and in one of his poems, 'Lines to William Cowper', Churchey recalled his 'intimacy from his earliest days' with 'my lov'd Henderson' (*ibid.* 106).

28 Barry, 'John Henderson (1757–1788)', n 1 above.

INDEX

A

A New Sett of Hymns and Psalm Tunes (James Leach, 1789) 67
Adam Clarke Portrayed (James Everett, 1843) 107
Agutter, William 108
An Earnest Appeal to Men of Reason and Religion (John Wesley, 1743) 35
Ancient and Modern: Hymns and Songs for Refreshing Worship (2013) 75
'And can it be that I should gain' (Charles Wesley) 77
Anti-Methodism 6–7, 11
apophatic and cataphatic processes 44–5
Arminian Magazine 88, 89, 102, 106
Armstrong, Karen 50
Asbury Theological Seminary 90, 93
Astley, J. 79

B

Baker, Frank 63–4
Battishill, Jonathan 76
Beacher, Henry 10
Beckerlegge, Oliver 64
Begbie, Jeremy 60–2, 64, 66, 67, 70, 76, 78
Bernard of Clairvaux 53
Bishop of Bristol 3
Bristol vii, 1–20
    1740 riots 11
    and John Henderson 98–100
Burke, Edmund x, 98, 99
Burstal (hymn tune) 67, 68

C

Calvinism vii, 1, 9, 11–12, 13, 15, 16, 17, 18, 19, 101, 109
Calvinistic Methodists 15, 16
Campbell, Ted A. 58–9, 78
Carr, Elizabeth 28
Cennick, John vii, 3, 4, 16
    and Wesleys 8–15, 16, 18
    and George Whitefield 14
Chapel and School Architecture (Frederick J. Jobson, 1850) 90

Charles Wesley's House, Bristol 85, 86
Charleston Hymnal, see *Psalms and Hymns*
Cheshire, Paul 99
Christ, Jesus 23, 28, 29, 30, 32, 34, 45, 46–7, 50, 51, 102
    Second Coming of viii, 21
'Christ the Lord is risen today' (Charles Wesley) 65–6
church (as community of faith) 34–7
    missional vision for 38
Church of England viii, 22, 35, 36, 71
Churchey, Walter 108–9
Clarke, Adam x, 106–7, 109
Claxton, Marshall 85, 92
Coleridge, Samuel Taylor, 98, 99
Collection of Hymns for the Use of the People Called Methodists (1780) 22, 25, 66
    fifth edition (1786) 67
colliers (of Kingswood) 1, 2, 3–4, 9, 11, 13, 15, 17, 87
Common Metre 67, 70, 75
Common Praise (2000) 75
Companion to the Wesleyan Hymnbook (1847) 68
conformance theory 60–1, 66
Connexion, John and Charles Wesley's vii, 82
Cook, Nicholas 60–1, 66, 76, 78
Cottle, Joseph 98, 99, 100, 101
Coward, Henry 71

D

Davie, Donald 45
de Joncourt, Robert 108
Dean, T. A. 86
Dionysius the Areopagite 44
'Directions for Singing' (John Wesley, 1761) 70
Dixon, Neil 65
Douglas, Richard Gilmore 85, 86, 90, 93

E

Early Fathers 44, 45
écriture see Kristeva, Julia

Index

Encoding Methodism: Telling and retelling narratives of Wesleyan origins (Ted A. Campbell, 2017) 58–9, 78

Epworth 62, 85, 86, 88

Eucharist 7, 10, 15, 46, 50, 53

evangelical revival viii, 1, 9, 14, 16, 18, 22, 35, 101, 110

evangelicalism 58, 77, 101, 110

Everett, James 82, 87, 107

F

Faber, Johann 88

Fellingham, Nathan 77

Fittler, J. 89

Forster, J. W. L. 91

Foundery Collection (John and Charles Wesley, 1742) 64, 65

Frost, Francis 46

Fry, W. T. 89

G

Gauntlett, Henry J. 70, 71

Gentleman's Magazine 98, 108

George II 33

Georgia 63

Gilbert, William 99, 100, 105

Goldberg, Brian 99

Gough, Richard 108

Green, Mrs 82, 84, 86

Gush, William 89–90

H

Handel, George Frederick 76

Hanham, Gloucestershire 10, 98, 100, 101, 104, 107

Harris, Howell 12, 15, 16

Haweis, Thomas 70, 72

Hempton, David 59–60

Henderson, John x, 97–113

and Bristol 98–100

and occult x, 98, 104–10

Henderson, Richard 98, 100, 107–8

and Wesleys 100

Hitch, Frederick Brook 93

Holy Club 63, 92

Holy Communion *see* Eucharist

Hudson, Thomas 84

Humphreys, Joseph 14

Huntingdon, Countess of 18, 85–6

hymns of Charles Wesley *see* Wesley, Charles

Hymns Ancient and Modern (1861, 1875) 71, 75

Hymns and Psalms (1983) 73, 75

Hymns and Sacred Poems (1739) 65

Hymns and Sacred Poems (1740) 66

Hymns and Sacred Poems (1742) 26

Hymns and Sacred Poems (1749) 29

Hymns and Spiritual Songs (1753) 67

I

Incarnation, doctrine of 32–3, 45–6, 48

J

Jackson, John 90, 92

Jackson, Thomas 82

Jesus *see* Christ

Jobson, Frederick J. 90

John Rylands Research Institute and Library, Manchester 83, 87, 88

John Wesley's House and Museum of Methodism 83, 86

Johnson, Ralph 92

Johnson, Samuel x, 98, 99

justice viii, 21, 31, 32, 110

justification (or salvation) by faith, doctrine of 4–5, 9

K

kenosis 51

Kershaw, John 89

Kimbrough, S T 46

kingdom of God 30–2

Kingswood 1, 2, 3–4, 8, 9, 12–13, 14, 15, 16, 18, 101, 107

Kingswood House 12, 15, 18

Kingswood School 90, 101, 106, 108

Kristeva, Julia 44, 53–5

on early human experiences 49–51

on *écriture* 48

L

Lampe, J. F. 76

Lely, Sir Peter 84

Let's Praise (1988) 73
Lightwood, James T. 70
Lydia (hymn tune) 72, 73, 75
Lyngham (hymn tune) 72, 73, 74, 75
Lyra Davidica (anon., 1708) 65

M

Macleane, Douglas 98
Madan, Martin 85
Manchester (hymn tune) 70, 71
Maquire, Patrick 88
Maxfield, Thomas 13
McIan, Robert Ronald 91
Methodism: Empire of the Spirit (David
　　Hempton, 2005) 59
Methodist Conference (1980) 75
Methodist people, the 36, 37
Mission Praise (1990) 73
Moravians ix, 9, 10, 17, 18, 46, 53, 63, 64
More, Hannah 98, 99, 100, 104
More, Henry 32
More, Patty 99
Music, Modernity, and God (Jeremy Begbie,
　　2013) 60

N

Nelson, John 4
New Room, Bristol vii, 3, 9, 10, 11, 12, 15,
　　16, 18, 85, 93
'New Version' *see* Tate and Brady
Nowers, Edward 10, 12, 13, 14

O

'O for a thousand tongues to sing' (Charles
　　Wesley) 66–76
Occult Philosophy (Heinrich Cornelius
　　Agrippa, 1533) 106
'Old Version' *see* Sternhold and Hopkins

P

Pembroke College, Oxford 98, 99
perfection, doctrine of vii, 1, 8–9, 10, 12,
　　13, 14, 15
Phatfish 77
pietism 59, 110
Portuguese earthquake (1755) 33
poverty 31–2

predestination, doctrine of 14, 17
Primitive Christianity 35, 36
Psalms and Hymns (John Wesley, 1737) 63

R

Rattenbury, J. E. 58
'renewal', in Charles Wesley's hymns 21–3,
　　24, 25, 27, 34
'restoration', in Charles Wesley's hymns
　　21–3, 24, 25, 26–38
revival *see* evangelical revival
'revival', in Charles Wesley's hymns 21–3
Richardson, Jonathan 84–5
Richmond (hymn tune) 70, 72, 73, 75
Ricoeur, Paul 43, 48, 55
Ridley, William 88
Riggall, Edward 87
Russell, John 81, 82, 84, 85–6

S

Sacred Harmony (1781) 67, 68
Sacred Melody (1761) 67
Sagina (hymn tune) 77
Salisbury, Frank O. 91
Salisbury Tune (hymn tune) 65
Savannah, Georgia 63
Sayce, Elizabeth 10
Scholes, Percy 68
Seward, William 12
shalom 31, 32, 35, 38
Shaw, Perry 30–1
Shury, J. 89
Simmonds (ship) 63
Singing the Faith (2011) 73
Smetham, James 90
Songs and Hymns of Fellowship (1987) 73
Southey, Robert 98, 99
Spilsbury, Jonathan 88
Sternhold and Hopkins, *The Whole Booke of
　　Psalmes* (1562) 62
Stonehouse, George 102
Stonehouse, James 98, 100
Symbolism, Christian 42–56
Sutcliffe, Joseph 4

T

Tate and Brady, *New Version of the Psalms
　　of David* (1696) 62

116

Index

The Character of a Methodist (John Wesley, 1742) 35
The Hurricane (William Gilbert, 1797) 99
The 'Lily Portrait' 84
The Methodist Hymn Book (1904) 71, 73
The Methodist Hymn Book (1933) 60, 72, 75
The Primitive Methodist Hymnal (1889) 70, 71
The Whole Booke of Psalmes (Thomas Este, 1592) 70
'Thoughts on the Power of Music' (John Wesley, 1781) 61
Tillich, Paul 43, 55
Trevecca 108, 109
Trewint Cottage, Cornwall 87
Trickett, Kenneth 73, 75
Trinity, the viii, 23, 24, 29, 47, 51
Tucker, Josiah 98, 100, 104, 105
Turner, Denys 44–5
Twelve Hymns, the Words by the Rev. Mr. Charles Wesley (Jonathan Battishill, 1765) 76
Twenty Four Hymns on the Great Festivals and Other Occasions (J. F. Lampe, 1746) 76

V
Valton, John 4
Vincent, Hobbes 93

W
Wallace, Charles 62
Ward, Graham 51
Watson, J. R. 58, 73, 75
Wesley, Charles vii
   and 1740 Bristol riots 11
   and Bristol 1–20
   early life and its impact 52–3, 62
   health issues 6, 10, 11
   hymns viii–x, 16, 21–41, 43–56, 57–80
   hymn-tunes ix–x
   and John Cennick 8, 11–15, 16–17
   and John Henderson x, 97–113
   musical experiences 62–4
   neologisms 47
   as pastor 6, 16
   pessimism 110

   portraits of x, 81–95
   and prayer 7
   preaching style 4–6
   use of metaphor 46–7
   use of paradox 45–6, 47
   and George Whitefield 1, 3, 5, 9, 10–11, 12, 14, 15, 16–17, 18, 19
Wesley, Charles Jr. 58, 81, 82, 85, 86, 87
Wesley, John vii
   achievements 18
   and Bristol 1–3, 9, 11, 12, 13, 16
   and John Cennick 8, 12–15, 17
   early life and its impact 52–3
   portraits of 81, 82, 85, 91
   preaching style 2–4, 5, 8
   'Thoughts on the Power of Music' (1781) 61
   and George Whitefield 1–3, 5, 9, 12, 14, 15, 16, 18
Wesley, Martha 84
Wesley, Samuel (father of Charles and John) 62, 84
Wesley, Samuel (son of Charles) 58, 81, 82, 85
Wesley, Sarah (or Sally, daughter of Charles) 82, 85, 86, 87, 97
   and John Henderson 100, 101, 105–6
Wesley, Sarah (wife of Charles) 85, 93
Wesley, Susanna 52, 62, 91
Wesley's Hymns and New Supplement (1876) 70
Wesleyan Methodist Magazine 90
Wesleyan Psalmist (1857) 68
Whelan, Tim 99–100
Whitefield, Elizabeth 9, 10–11
Whitefield, George vii, 10–11, 14, 15, 16, 86
   and Bristol 1–3
   preaching style 5
   Tabernacles 16, 17
   and Wesleys 1–3, 12, 14, 15, 16, 18, 19
Whitehead, John 4, 89
Wilberforce, William x, 86, 99, 100
Williams, John Michael 84
Williams, Joseph 5–6
Wiltshire (hymn tune) 68, 69
Winchester Old (hymn tune) 70, 71

Y
Young, Carlton R. 62

117

ISBN   978-1-83772-195-5
eISBN   978-1-83772-196-2
ISSN (Print)   2057-4517
ISSN (Online)   2057-4525
The Journal of Religious History, Literature and Culture
© University of Wales Press, 2024
Articles and reviews © The Contributors, 2024

Printed by CPI Group (UK) Ltd

Contributors to *The Journal of Religious History, Literature and Culture* should refer enquiries to the journal page at *www.uwp.co.uk* or e-mail press@press.wales.ac.uk requesting notes for contributors.

Advertising enquiries should be sent to the Sales and Marketing Department at the University of Wales Press, at the address below.

Subscriptions: *The Journal of Religious History, Literature and Culture* is published twice a year in June and November. The annual subscription for institutions is £95 (print only), £85 (online only) or £140 (combined); and for individuals is £25 (print or online only) or £40 (combined). Subscription orders should be sent to University of Wales Press, University Registry, King Edward VII Avenue, Cardiff CF10 3NS. E-mail: press@press.wales.ac.uk.

Open Access: The University of Wales Press (UWP) is fully committed to the principle of Open Access for those authors requiring it, whether by funder mandate, REF or otherwise. It is incumbent on contributors to state clearly if they have an Open Access requirement when submitting an article.

UWP's policy is to require an embargo period of eighteen months for Green Open Access, to begin on the last day in the month of publication of the print version. We also welcome submissions for Gold Open Access: if required, please contact the Commissioning Department at UWP to discuss an Article Processing Charge (APC) for your article.

The version of record for deposit should be the author's accepted and final peer-reviewed text, for non-commercial purposes.

The inclusion of third-party material in the deposited article will be at the author/institution's own risk. Authors should continue to ensure clearance of rights for third-party material for print and e-publication in the usual way for the purposes of the version published by UWP and for Open Access, if your article is Open Access.

UWP will continue to accept and publish articles by authors without requirements for REF under pre-existing arrangements.

For more information on our current Open Access policy, please visit our website: *www.uwp.co.uk/open-access*.